IT'S NOT HOW YOU LOOK,
IT'S WHAT YOU SEE

LISA BEVERE

CHARISMA
HOUSE

Cover design by Lisa Rae Cox, Justin Evans, Allan Nygren
Design Director: Justin Evans

Visit the author's website at www.messengerinternational.org.

Library of Congress Cataloging-in-Publication Data
Bevere, Lisa.
  It's not how you look, it's what you see / by Lisa Bevere.
      pages cm
  Includes bibliographical references and index.
  ISBN 978-1-62998-030-0 (trade paper : alk. paper) -- ISBN 978-1-62998-198-7 (e-book : alk. paper)
  1. Christian women--Religious life. 2. Body image in women--Religious aspects--Christianity. I. Title.
    BV4527.B4944 2014
    248.8'43--dc23
                                        2014024969

Portions of this book were previously published as *The True Measure of a Woman* by Charisma House, ISBN 978-1-59979-150-0, copyright © 1997, 2007 and *You Are Not What You Weigh* by Charisma House, ISBN 978-1-59979-075-6, copyright © 1998, 2007.

14 15 16 17 18 — 9 8 7 6 5 4 3 2
Printed in the United States of America

What do you see with your eyes closed?
Do you see dreams and hopes, or do
you see nightmares and failures?

As I've journeyed through life, I've proved this
truth: what you see with an open heart is far more
important than what you see with open eyes.

We are in a day and age when an inordinate
amount of significance is placed on how people
look and with whom they are seen. Both of
these are fleeting, fickle dynamics destined
to shift in our ever-changing world. I have
penned this book in the hope of anchoring
you to the hope of the unseen eternal.

You are more than what you see, what
you've done, or who you've known. You
are destined for the unseen realm that far
outweighs all that you could imagine!

—LISA BEVERE

CONTENTS

1 It's Not About Being Seen, It's What You See.................. 1

2 The Tyrant 15

3 The Image of the Truth 31

4 The Image of the Lie...................................... 45

5 Self-Image or Self-Worship?........................... 57

6 The Idol Tumbles.. 71

7 Sharpening Your Spiritual Sight 83

8 Tearing Down Idols.. 95

9 Escaping Your Past 105

10 What You See 119

 Appendix: Signs of Eating Disorders........................... 127

 Notes... 129

Chapter 1

IT'S NOT ABOUT BEING SEEN, IT'S WHAT YOU SEE

Everything we hear is an opinion, not a fact.
Everything we see is a perspective, not the truth.[1]
—MARCUS AURELIUS

Do you know that how you see is far more important than how you look? I do, and yet for me, walking this out is a dance of daily recalibration. You see, rearranging the furniture of my life or altering my physical appearance is so much easier than daily lifting my sight.

Appearance is how you and I are seen or perceived by others. As much as we have the freedom to change the way we look, we have little to almost no control over how others choose to see us.

No matter how attractive, well-positioned, or social media savvy you are, someone is going to choose to dislike you. Regardless of how good your intentions are in family, work, or fashion, someone will find a reason to misread or misinterpret. The truth is, *misunderstanding* will happen more readily than *understanding*. It is frustrating but true.

You can't control how you are seen, but you can choose how you see. While my appearance is how my world sees me, how I see becomes my vantage point on my world. Looks are about being seen. But more than being seen, our world needs you to see. It needs you to open wide your eyes.

Perspective has the power to distort or enhance, dismiss or embrace.

Not long ago, at the start of a new year, I wrote a blog post about fasting that featured some of the concepts in this book—only to be shocked by the response. I opened with this statement:

> A diet changes the way you look. A fast changes the way you see.

To say this concept resonated would be an understatement. It became glaringly apparent that people were tired of simply looks and looking; they were desperate to see. Below is an excerpt of the blog post that accompanied this statement.

> Perhaps you feel a bit like me: holiday hung-over from a bit too much of *a bit too much*. I look like I need to give birth to a Christmas food baby. Good thing it's January, right? It's time for that annual fast and some serious New Year resolutions.
>
> But wait. What if instead of a diet/fast combo I really pressed into a bit more? Rather than simply changing how I look, I want to change how I see.
>
> I truly sense that the year before us will require a heightened sense of sight. We will need greater vision to see us through. Rather than allowing the cross that loomed before Him to fill His eyes, Jesus saw through the cross to the joy set before Him (see Hebrews 12:2). How about you?
>
> Are there some areas you need to see through?
>
> Are you tired of being limited to how you look?
>
> Are you ready to be released by what you see?
>
> I certainly hope so. Your family, your friends, and this world need you to connect with a larger vision than what you've seen.

My sense of our need for renewed sight has carried long past the day I wrote that blog post. That is why I felt it was time to delve a bit deeper and revise and update something that had already been written.

I wrote the book *You Are Not What You Weigh* more than a decade ago, and as time has passed, I have met women who have found liberty as God's Word brought light into formerly shadowed realms. Women who were once captive to an eating disorder are now strong and free. For some, the release was nearly immediate. In a short span of days they saw everything differently and were able to move into the largeness of a new life. (That is the power of what you see!)

As I revisit the words I wrote years ago, it is my desire that the same kind of encounter with truth will set you free from any captivity of vision. What formerly addressed issues of body image and weight has grown into a larger story about how you see. It is my earnest prayer that these pages will unlock your sight and lift your vision.

RENEWED SIGHT

When I first started wearing glasses, I argued with the optometrist, "These are too strong! I can see *everything*!"

"You're supposed to," he countered.

"No, you don't understand," I insisted. "I can see leaves on the trees!"

I had gotten used to my poor vision and the soft, blurry world I had been perceiving. Trees were brown trunks with soft, shimmering green blobs on top. I had been expecting that once my vision was corrected, I would see these same images magnified, not clarified.

However, with corrected eyesight, instead of being magnified, my world seemed smaller and less private. I noticed the *people* in cars, not just the cars. I wondered how often people I knew had been waving to me, only to find their friendly greetings returned with blank stares.

My eyes had been veiled by nearsighted vision. When the veil was removed, I saw clearly—sometimes more clearly than I wished. I had enjoyed the soft-focus-lens look of my face. Now in the hard light of reality, I saw every freckle and pore. Looking in the mirror one day, I asked my husband, "Is this how you see me?"

"Is *what* how I see you?" he asked, looking perplexed.

"Can you see *this*?" I asked as I pointed to a brown spot on my face.

"Yes."

"Can you see *this*?" I asked, pointing to a blemish.

"Yes."

"Have you always seen these? I don't like the way I look when I can see," I murmured as I turned from the mirror and pulled off my glasses.

John came around behind me and turned me back toward the mirror. "Do you want me to tell you what I see?"

I really did, but in response, I just shrugged my shoulders. "Put your glasses on and look in the mirror," John ordered.

While standing behind me, he pointed out to me what he saw each time he looked at me. He highlighted all the things he liked about my features. My focus shifted from the flaws to the love that overlooked them. As I looked closer I saw the good that John saw in me.

Just like me with my new glasses, when you first turned from your sins and beheld your true image, you probably didn't like what you saw—the remnants of the flaws, wrinkles, and blemishes of your former life. The clarification brought magnification to your shortcomings.

With my glasses, I came to a new realization: *my flaws had always been there, but I had been loved in spite of them.* It's the same for you. Your flaws have always been there, but God loves you in spite of them.

Today's culture—even church culture when it is legalistic and religious—is constantly attempting to focus on your flaws instead of your true worth. Unknowingly, you can allow cultural influences to drape, disfigure, and mask what God has done. You can easily lose sight of the truth.

The Lord wants to call you out of your cold, dark hiding place into the gentle warmth of the light of the knowledge of Him. Perhaps you are afraid to come into His presence, afraid the way will be barred by mistakes you have made since you have been a Christian. You are afraid your works are not good enough or numerous enough to grant you entrance. You are afraid that if you call, He will not answer. So you hide in fear of rejection, assuming it is better not to try than to be disappointed. You don't reach out, fearing you will be turned away.

I'm writing this book to remind you that you have nothing to hide. You have boldness because of Christ. God wants you to be confident as you come before Him in your time of need. He wants you to be transformed even more than you want to be. He longs to speak to you more than you even want to hear from Him. He is waiting for you to turn to Him so He can remove anything in your heart that may be separating you from glorious intimacy with Him!

WEIGHTS AND MEASURES

Our world is constantly trying to tell you what determines your value—and sell you something that will increase your worth according to that standard. God offers another scale.

A scale measures weight or rate of exchange, matching value for value and worth for worth. For example, if a dollar buys a quarter of a pound of jellybeans, you would place a quarter-pound weight on one side of the scale and add jellybeans to the other side until both sides balanced.

An honest scale is a symbol of justice, representing equality, equity, and fairness. When a scale is balanced, it is considered to be just. When a scale of justice is unbalanced, it has been tipped unfairly in one direction by influence or deceptive weights. Its calculations are no longer trustworthy.

We have all heard the saying "worth its weight in gold." This saying has its origins in ancient times, when valuables were placed on just such a scale and weighed in proportion to an identical measure of purest gold.

I believe this concept has both a practical and a spiritual application. To better understand the spiritual application we must first gain a good understanding of its natural application.

In ancient times, vendors would tinker with scales and misrepresent weights to take advantage of their customers. For example, if you were to request one pound of flour from a dishonest vendor, he would place the lightened version of a one-pound weight on one side of the scale and your flour on the other side.

As you watched, he would add or deduct flour until the scales appeared to balance. Your flour would be transferred into a sack or container, and you'd be sent on your way. As you walked away, you would have no way of knowing that your sack was shy a few ounces of flour.

You would have been certain the measure of it was accurate. After all, you watched just to make sure—but the merchant's one-pound balance weight actually weighed just fourteen ounces. You paid for more flour than you received.

In this manner merchants were able to increase their profit margin. When you went home and dumped what you thought was a pound of flour into your recipe for bread, you found out there was a problem. The only way to avoid this sort of theft was to go to a reputable source and make accurate weights of your own. But even using your own weights, the merchants would argue that their weights were right and yours were too heavy.

DECEITFUL GAIN

Merchants also used this practice when they purchased grain from farmers. For their suppliers they had another set of weights. These weights were heavier than what they actually represented. For example, a one-pound weight might really weigh eighteen ounces. Farmers would sell their grain to the merchants to market, usually in large quantities. A measure that was off just a little would mean great profit to the merchant and great loss to the unaware farmer.

In ancient times, the only way to avoid this sort of deception was to have your own method of weighing your goods before you brought them to market. It is no different today. If you don't have any accurate appraisal of your worth, you will sell out for far less. It's important not to accept the worth the enemy says you possess. You must know the authority and position you have through Jesus.

Dishonest weights will also cause you to sell yourself short. If you accept culture's measure, or value, as accurate, you will never know you've been undersold.

To counteract this deception, you will need to go to an honest source and get some accurate measuring weights, ones that have not been tampered with or hollowed out by the merchants of this world.

AN ACCURATE MEASURE

Our search is for an accurate measure, one that balances truth and worth. It must be pure, incorruptible, solid, and tested. There is only one source to find this type of measure. It is found in the treasury of God's counsel and wisdom. Once you find this measure, you must use it to assure that you will never again be sold something less valuable.

This measure will consist of truth. For it is *God's truth* that sets you free. Let's pattern this quest for truth after Solomon's search. Although he was the wisest man ever to live, he was the first to admit he did not hold within himself the answers.

Solomon set his mind on the pursuit of wisdom and to understand the meaning behind everything God had made. As a king who reigned during peaceful times, he was able to devote himself entirely to this endeavor. It is interesting to note that this was his quest even after God appeared to Solomon in a dream:

> The LORD appeared to Solomon during the night in a dream, and God said, "Ask for whatever you want me to give you."
>
> —1 KINGS 3:5

Can you imagine the intensity of this moment? What if Solomon's heart had not been prepared? I've said and done some pretty wild stuff in my dreams. Solomon might have asked for a "good thing" yet missed the "God thing." He could have asked that Jerusalem would prosper and that his kingdom would expand. He could have asked for the health of his children and wives.

But he did not.

Solomon's request was a reflection of what God desired in the king of Israel. He answered:

> Give your servant a discerning heart to govern your
> people and to distinguish between right and wrong.
> For who is able to govern this great people of yours?
> —1 Kings 3:9

This was not the answer of a know-it-all. Solomon was
humbled by the gargantuan task set before him. The Lord
was pleased with Solomon's response. So God blessed him
with even more:

> Since you have asked for this and not for long life or
> wealth for yourself, nor have asked for the death of
> your enemies but for discernment in administering
> justice, I will do what you have asked. I will give
> you a wise and discerning heart, so that there will
> never have been anyone like you, nor will there ever
> be. Moreover, I will give you what you have not
> asked for—both riches and honor—so that in your
> lifetime you will have no equal among kings.
> —1 Kings 3:11–13

GAINING WISDOM

Not only would Solomon be the wisest man who had ever
lived, but he also would rise above his peers—and his
wisdom would outlive him to surpass the wisdom of all
future generations of kings and leaders. For all our technology and instant access to the Internet, Solomon was
still wiser. He had none of our high-tech resources to draw
from, but he drew from the counsel of the Creator and
therefore he was wiser.

At first this claim might seem unbelievable, but you can be certain it is indeed the truth because it was made by God. If you are awed by how this could possibly be true, it is because you are using a flawed measurement of wisdom.

There is a mistaken impression that the accumulation of knowledge is wisdom. If this were indeed true, to what lofty pinnacle has this vast knowledge brought us? We live in a culture brimming with excess, poverty, perversion, violence, and wickedness. Ours is a generation of people who are self-ruled and haughty. Our world is riddled with disease, plague, want, and war. It is obvious that in our pursuit of knowledge we have forsaken truth.

Without wisdom we may possess all the knowledge this world may offer and still remain fools. It is not more technology or knowledge that we need. Our souls cry out for wisdom. Wisdom is the ability to apply knowledge, experience, and truth while retaining proper relationship with God and man.

Wisdom gives us eyes to see and ears to hear. Only then will we recognize truth when we find it. In the pursuit of knowledge we have strayed from the path of wisdom and discretion. We have allowed knowledge to exalt us to the realm of self-rule. We have become a generation of self-ruled, self-motivated *fools.* "The fool says in his heart, 'There is no God'" (Psalm 14:1). Many people acknowledge God's existence while they live as though He does not.

Solomon sensed his overwhelming need for wisdom. As ruler of God's people, he bore more than a national government upon his shoulders. He set his heart to make wisdom his lifelong pursuit. He held a royal position in which his riches were unfathomable, his influence worldwide, and his authority and power were respected and feared. Kings from all over the world brought tribute to Solomon in deference to his wisdom and excellence.

Though you don't have the resources of Solomon, his wisdom is recorded so that you might continually benefit from it. And even more, you have access to the One who was the source of all Solomon's insights.

IN SEARCH OF THE TRUTH

I believe God awakens an inquisitive questioning in you when He wants you to go searching for answers. To learn, you must first ask questions. Questions are not always comfortable, but they are necessary. Throughout this book I'm going to ask you questions and I don't want you to skip over them! I want you to take time to search inside yourself for honest answers. Ask God to shine a light on the areas of your heart that you've been afraid to examine. With His love and grace, you can face anything you discover about yourself along your journey.

It's important that I ask these questions—even knowing that you cannot hear my voice and I cannot hear your answer. Through these pages, you and I can communicate on a more intimate, unspoken level—one that would not be possible even if we were face-to-face.

I don't presume to know all of life's answers, but this book is from my heart to yours, and I believe it bears a glimpse of our Father's heart, too. Through its quiet pages, we will talk—and it is my prayer that the power of the Holy Spirit will overshadow all we discuss so that together we may glean His wisdom.

As you turn these pages and read the truth of God, He will remove the scales that kept you from seeing. Let His light illuminate your eyes.

Pray with me:

> *Father God,*
>
> *Reveal Your truth to me by Your Word and Spirit. Lord, give me eyes to see, ears to hear, and a heart that perceives and understands. Above all these, Lord, grant me a willing and pliable heart that will believe and apply Your truth so that it may bring forth Your fruit in my life. I give You permission to change my perspective. Reveal Yourself, for You are the way, the truth, and the life. Amen.*

Believe that He will.

Chapter 2

THE TYRANT

To rise from error to truth is rare and beautiful.[1]

—Victor Hugo

HAVE YOU EVER stopped to think about the power you give to whatever you believe? It's true. Once believed, a lie's power in your life will grow and grow until it becomes a tyranny.

Tyranny is a very strong word that describes an actual stronghold. It describes a process of thinking so oppressive and hopeless that those under its domain soon become depressed and disillusioned. Those under tyranny are held captive beneath the heavy weight of constant failure, pressure, and accusation. Tyranny creates a bondage so far-reaching that its tentacles are felt in every area of life.

I want to radically interrupt your torment. I believe you can be free from the bondage of any tyrant that holds you captive—whether it's a lie you've believed about your appearance, fear, pride, unbelief, disobedience, addiction, or something else. Your outward condition reflects a deeper inner turmoil. This captivity did not start on your exterior frame or in your external circumstances. It began in secret, deep within, and it has worked its destruction *from the inside out.*

It could have been last year, five years ago, or a very long time ago when those deep-seated lies were whispered into the inner recesses of your mind. At first you thought the voice was a friend. So you listened. Its helpful hints kept you in check.

Then came the comparisons. Then the whispered accusations that progressed into a critical, nagging obsession. Soon you were not only listening—you were believing. Deception spread from the realm of your thought life and spilled out until it wove itself into the very fibers of your being, affecting your insights and your actions. It may have even distorted the visual perception of your eyes so that now all you see in the mirror is failure. It continues its constant conversation of correction and comparison in your mind. The voice harasses and accuses you daily.

Before we go further, I want you to answer some questions honestly. Don't give the answers you think sound right; there is no one grading this, and you will only cheat yourself if you are not 100 percent honest. As you listen for answers you may hear two voices with conflicting opinions. So listen with your heart, not your head.

> *Do you recognize the voice I have just described?*

> *How loud is it? Do you hear it even when others are talking to you?*

> *How often does it interrupt your thoughts: monthly, weekly, daily, hourly, or more often?*

> *What does it say to you?*

> *Are these the words and descriptions of a friend?*

> *Do you believe them?*

> *Can you silence the voice?*

I want to share a truth with you: *what holds you captive in the natural is rooted in the spiritual.* It has grown from a seed, a word, a disapproving glance, a rejection, or a comparison. It was planted deep into the soil of a wound in your soul during a time (or many times) when rejection or acceptance of you as a person was based on your physical form, relationships, success, or some other faulty measure. Or perhaps it was planted during a time when your person was violated in such a painful way that you decided to barricade yourself physically from the world rather than endure that kind of pain again. Or perhaps you just bowed under the weight of the constant barrage of negative, accusing messages sent by advertising and negligent entertainment media.

Each story is different, but I want to share *my* story, the liberation God has brought from my former struggle with an eating disorder. There is nothing more powerful than the shared one-on-one testimony of what God has done in our lives. I cannot be there personally with you, but through the pages of this book I believe you will hear what I have to say in a very deep and personal way.

Even as I revisit and recount this period of my life, it is hard to imagine I once lived under such captivity. It is now a gray, dark, and distant shadow—almost unreal in contrast to the light and freedom Jesus has brought.

This same freedom waits for you. You may not struggle with an eating disorder, but you picked up this book because you know, in some way, there's disorder in your life. Though your condition and circumstances may vary from mine, God's truth remains steadfast and absolute. It is His deepest desire not only to set you free, but also to banish your deepest and darkest fears. He seeks to restore and reassign value to the precious, to discard the vile, and to breathe life, hope, and direction where there has been discouragement, death, and confusion.

As you seek to reorder the disorder of your life, I pray that the principles God taught me in my own time of reordering will help you also to win the victory. Perhaps you will recognize someone you know and love in my story. Maybe you will even glimpse a reflection of yourself in my words.

MY TYRANT

There was a six-year period in my life when weight dominated my thoughts. I want to take you back there with me. My struggle began years before I became a Christian, yet it continued after I'd become one. It was important enough to God to set me free, and it is a very real account of the gospel of my life. It is an area where the Word of God was truly made flesh.

Until I was sixteen years of age, I had little or no awareness of my body weight. I was only weighed at summer camp (to make certain I wasn't losing weight on a diet of camp food) and at physicals to establish a pattern of growth. I perceived any increase in my weight in the same way I viewed any increase in my height—a sign of maturing.

I was small for my age and always very active, swimming competitively nearly year round on one team or another from the time I was five. With this lifestyle I could eat whatever I wanted, whenever I wanted, without a thought about my weight.

In my sophomore year of high school, I decided to run hurdles following swimming season. During the first week of practice, I snapped my Achilles tendon and had to be on crutches for a while. I decided not to swim during my junior year in order to allow my ankle to heal. All sports stopped, but I still ate as though I were in training.

One day as I walked into the house from school, my father stopped me and looked me over disapprovingly. "Come over here and turn around," he said. "Boy, those jeans are tight! How much do you weigh?"

"One hundred twenty-eight." Frightened, I had volunteered my summer camp weight. The truth was I had no idea what I now weighed.

"There is no way you weigh that! You're at least one hundred thirty-five pounds, and probably one forty!" he challenged. "Go weigh yourself."

I was sure he was wrong, but I wandered into my parents' bathroom and stepped onto the scale. To my disbelief I weighed one hundred thirty-eight pounds!

Ashamed, I reported back to my father. He told me I was much too big. He warned me about how my weight would affect my desirability as a young girl. Who would want to ask me out if I was fat?

I went to my room to look at myself, really inspecting my body for the first time. I struggled to pull off my jeans—obviously they were too tight! I could see the seam lines and, in some places, even the stitches running up and down my legs. The imprints of the waistband and pockets were embedded around my midriff. I stripped down to my bra and underwear and stood on my bed so I could see my body. My view was limited to my shoulders down.

I looked at the headless reflection and really hated what I saw. I needed to punish it and take it back under my control.

"You're gross and fat!" I chided.

I berated myself as I grabbed the various parts of my body, all of which appeared grossly out of proportion. I repeated the ritual on my backside, then childishly bounced off my bed.

I went over to my closet, pulled out my swimming sweats, and put them on. I felt better immediately in loose clothes. I felt safe and hidden. Now it was time to inspect my closet. What else was too tight? I pulled the clothes out and tried on different items. Each time something was tight, even if it was something I had simply outgrown, I walked over to the mirror and punished my reflection: "You look fat! You *are* fat!" I didn't know it at the time, but in those moments I was changing my identity from *who I was* to *what I looked like*.

That night under the watchful eye of my father, I denied myself second helpings and dessert. After dinner I pulled on a down coat over my sweats and ran the snowdrifts until I felt as though my lungs would burst from the cold winter air. I was determined to lose the weight and get back to one hundred twenty-eight pounds.

The next day at lunch I cut back again. At dinner each night I cut back on my portions, and after dinner I ran.

I pored over articles in my mother's magazines that gave information on weight loss and dieting.

In two weeks I had lost ten pounds. Everyone at school noticed. Even some of the upperclassmen complimented my weight loss. I felt powerful. I had conquered my body. I was in charge of my weight. I would never be fat again. I swam again during my senior year, and I grew an inch, reaching five feet seven inches. My weight whittled down to a muscular one hundred twenty-five pounds. It seemed as if my weight problems were far behind me.

After graduation, I chose a college far from my home-town in Indiana. I wanted to break away from all that was familiar. I wanted to experience the West, so I traveled to the University of Arizona. I went through sorority rush and pledged a house even before school began. Now I had built-in friends.

I couldn't help noticing all my sorority sisters were tan, thin, beautiful, and blonde (at least the majority were blonde). Suddenly I felt awkward and clumsy among these svelte Barbie lookalikes in ponytails. As I compared myself with my newly acquired Californian and Arizonan sorority sisters, my one-hundred-twenty-five-pound body looked like an Indiana corn-fed heifer next to a racehorse. I tried not to draw comparisons, but it was evident every-where I looked.

At dinner girls who were thinner than me would com-plain, "I'm so fat! Just look at these thighs!"

I would, and I realized their thighs were smaller than mine. If they were fat, then I was *obese*!

"How much do you weigh?" I asked one girl.

"One hundred fifteen pounds."

"Oh, you're thin. You're not fat!" I protested.

She jumped up from the table and grabbed the back of her thigh. "Look at all this cottage cheese! I *am* fat."

I felt foolish. I could only see the fat because she had grabbed her thigh in a vice grip. I remained silent as I scooted further under the table and prayed that no one would ask my weight. I was ten pounds heavier than her. It never crossed my mind that I was also three inches taller.

That night in the privacy of my dorm room I checked my own thighs. There it was! I had cottage-cheese fat too! Maybe she had been hinting about my fat so I would lose weight.

I began to swim and run again. I stopped eating the cafeteria sandwiches at lunch, eating only the salad. I dropped my weight several pounds to one hundred twelve. But still I did not feel thin enough.

At every meal we all discussed the caloric count for each item on our plates. The one who knew the most about dieting was the smartest. We ruthlessly confessed and pointed out our flaws to each other: "Look at my stomach; isn't it disgusting!" we'd complain as we lifted our shirts for inspection.

"Well, look at this!" another would counter as she pinched her young, taut, tan legs, looking for a flaw.

My stomach was flat, my thighs were tan and thin, and my arms were muscular and trim, but I had a flaw.

My flaw was my face. Each time I looked in the mirror I saw failure. My jaw is square, and no matter how thin I got it still looked wide. I would stare in the mirror, and all I could see was a huge, fat face staring back. I would critically assess myself as though I were an enemy. "I'll get rid of these jowls!" I would say as I grabbed my lower cheeks. At one point during my junior year, I was a size one and weighed only one hundred three pounds. Still my face looked fat when I looked in the mirror. It was all I could see. I didn't notice the gauntness or the veins that laced my neck. My focus was so distorted.

I also had another person in my life who reinforced my warped impression. My boyfriend constantly commented about my face, monitoring my weight carefully. At the time I thought he just wanted me to be the best I could be, but the truth is, he did it to control me.

When I went home for Christmas my mother was alarmed by how much weight I had lost. She was so concerned that she took me to the doctor. He assured her I was still within the safety limits for my height, but when my mother left the room, he asked me if I was trying to lose the weight.

"No, it is just too hot to eat," I assured him. This was a partial truth. Arizona was considerably hotter, and heavy foods did sound uncomfortable.

"Well, just make sure you take care of yourself. Maybe you should get up in the middle of the night and eat a steak!" he winked.

I smiled and finished getting dressed, although the very thought of steak revolted me.

That night my mother made my favorite meal.

"I'm not hungry," I told her when she encouraged me to eat.

"You have to eat!" she insisted.

"I'll eat later with my friends; I'm going to a party tonight," I replied. "We'll get pizza."

"You need something healthy. You've hardly eaten all day!" my mother answered.

She was right. I had hardly eaten. I was afraid that by coming home I would get fat again. I thought everyone was trying to force food on me. "They just don't want me thin," I thought to myself. "They're against me. They don't want me to succeed."

My mom tried to enlist my father's support. "Tell her to eat."

"She'll be fine." He looked up from his paper and smiled at me.

I knew my new weight had won his approval. At least he wouldn't push me to eat!

I went out that night with my new and improved, tan Arizona body. I felt like a different person. I walked and talked like my sorority sisters. I had learned something else from them too—how to party! I flitted around the party, drawing strength from this newfound attention.

"You look great! I should have asked you to the prom!" one boy exclaimed.

Wow! Was this real, or was it a dream? Boys who had

never given me a second glance in high school were now asking me out. Later that night, as I lay in bed, I determined never to go back to what I had been before.

When I got back to college I realized I had gained some of my weight back. While complaining to a sorority sister about it, she suggested taking water retention pills. I remembered my mother taking them, but I wasn't sure what they were for. "Isn't that just for before your period?" I asked.

"No!" she assured me. "I take them every Friday morning so I'll be thin by Friday night!"

It sounded too good to be true. "Are you sure they are OK?" I asked.

"Yes, look—they are not even prescription!" She handed me a box of diuretic pills that looked harmless. The front of the box sported a picture of a happy woman in a bikini. I flipped them over and read the ingredients.

"They've got a lot of caffeine."

"Yeah, it is great. Caffeine gives you a buzz! Try one."

I put one in my pocket. I'd always been able to lose weight easily before. I'd lose it again. But this time it was taking longer.

Meals were getting harder for me to resist. I thought more and more about *food*—not just about my weight. I developed a passion for food and for drinking. I loved everything to the extreme. If I drank, I drank to get drunk. If I ate, I ate until I was engorged and uncomfortable. But I still wanted to get attention for my looks, so I exercised to the extreme. In a constant pursuit to burn calories, I never sat still. I would even shake my legs all through classes or during my study time. I ate excessively—or dieted excessively. There was no in-between. I only thought about school when I had a test. Still, I retained a B average.

The law of food restriction had aroused an excessive desire in me. The law always enflames the lusts of the flesh and soul. I could starve myself, but once I started eating there was no stopping until physically I could eat no more or the food was gone. It was either feast or famine.

This is a hard lifestyle to maintain, and I enlisted the help of laxatives, then diuretics, in my battle. By my junior year in college, my body was addicted to them. It no longer functioned normally. Coupled with a stomach disorder I already had, I was in constant discomfort. I was afraid of my own body. "What if I couldn't go to the bathroom? What if I got fat?"

I became ill and began to run a constant low-grade fever. A rash broke out all over my upper body. Finally I went to the school infirmary. "How long has it been since your last bowel movement?" the doctor asked, looking concerned as she poked my stomach.

"A month. But usually I go once a week," I assured her.

She shook her head in disbelief. "Honey, you should go nearly every day. We are going to have to do some tests on you."

First they X-rayed me. The results showed that my intestines were backed up to my lungs. Immediately they checked me into the hospital under the care of a specialist. It was a nightmare. They gave me a prescription-strength laxative; when that didn't work, they made me drink a tumbler full of castor oil. The cramping was horrible.

Then I was subjected to a series of enemas, then more tests. I was finally diagnosed with irritable bowel syndrome and severe lactose intolerance. The whole ordeal shook me up so much that I stopped taking laxatives and diuretics. But still I was obsessed with my weight.

At dinner I watched one of my sorority sisters eat. She consumed everything on her plate and then some. She wasn't fat. How did she do it? I never saw her running or exercising. In private I asked her the secret.

"I eat everything I want, then I go into the bathroom and stick my toothbrush handle down my throat. Then I brush my teeth."

She made it sound so easy.

"Can you show me how?" I asked.

"Sure! After dinner tonight, just come and brush your teeth with me."

That night after dinner I followed her ponytailed form upstairs to our common bathroom. For the first time I noticed a lot of my sorority sisters walking into the stalls with toothbrushes in their hand.

"Just go in and do it," she said.

I hesitated; I hated throwing up. Did I really want to do this? She smiled and shrugged at me as if to say, "Whatever," and slipped into the privacy of her stall. I listened. It didn't really sound like throwing up, more like choking or coughing. "Did you—?"

"Yes, it is that easy."

I bravely stepped in my stall and knelt down in front of the toilet. Before this moment, I had only knelt when I prayed my childhood bedtime prayers. Now I was kneeling before a toilet like it was an idol. I jumped to my feet.

"I can't do it," I protested.

"Sure you can. I do it all the time." She encouraged me with the voice of a cheerleader. I closed my eyes, pushed the toothbrush handle toward the back of my throat, and gagged.

"It didn't work!"

"Try again."

I gagged again. My eyes began to water. I stood up. "I can't do this," I thought. "I'll just have to starve myself or think of something else." The school year was almost over, and I was still thinner than most of the girls back home in Indiana. I'd figure something out that summer.

By now I was hopelessly chained to the disorder of my weight and food obsession. It would take more than my frantic attempts to learn how to reorder this area of my life.

YOUR TYRANT

Does any of this sound familiar to what's been happening in your own life? Perhaps your issue is not with eating or body image but with success, money, relationships, possessions, or something else. Even now an area of disorder may be coming to mind, highlighted by God's Spirit.

Consider the following questions:

ઠ *In what area has the enemy established a stronghold to keep you captive?*

ઠ *Are you ready to be free from this tyranny?*

If so, I invite you now on a journey to freedom. The
first step is an encounter with the image of the truth.

Chapter 3

THE IMAGE OF THE TRUTH

People only see what they are prepared to see.[1]
—RALPH WALDO EMERSON

A T THIS POINT, you have identified and declared war on the tyrant that has oppressed you. But how can one resist and overcome such influences? How can wounds so deep and secret ever be healed? You must first *know who you really are*. As a human, you are created in the image of God, and there are multiple dimensions of you.

> Then God said, "Let us make man in our image, in our likeness..." So God created man in his own image, in the image of God he created him; male and female he created them.
> —GENESIS 1:26–27

First, there is the physical or natural dimension of you. It is what you see when you look in the mirror. It is the image reflected and projected to others. It functions in conjunction with the five senses. It sees, smells, tastes, hears, and touches. It is the outer shell that houses you. It protects, nourishes, grows, reproduces, ages, and eventually dies.

This physical realm can be broken, scarred, wounded, healed, and strengthened. To some degree it can be altered, but physically you and I are the product of a genetic compilation passed down through centuries of reproduction. Your physical body is not unlike a fruit tree, which grows from seed form to full maturity. You pass through stages of growth and harvest, each varying in their timing and season.

Your physical body in itself is a testament to the glory of God. For all of man's years of study, it is still a mystery.

Man cannot create; he can only clone, or re-create, human life. Man cannot *produce* life; he can merely *reproduce*.

A creator originates what others duplicate. God is the Creator of all life. He is the Creator of your individual life and physical form. He was intimately involved in each and every detail. Surely you have witnessed the miracle and wonder of a baby. It is the very handiwork of God.

You can look at a baby and see the miracle, but can you look at yourself today and say the same? Can you call yourself fearfully and wonderfully made? Or is the wonder crowded out by a list of shortcomings and flaws?

Your physical self, though the most obvious, is the least representative of the real you. The physical can only touch physically. You cannot physically reach within yourself and touch your soul, yet *that* is the real you.

Though you cannot touch it and though you've never seen it, you know your soul is there. The soul has a range of senses all its own. It is the part of you that *feels*—not physically but emotionally. In your soul you experience happiness, sadness, joy, and pain. If you were ever made fun of, it was your soul—not your physical body—that experienced the pain.

The soul consists of your mind, will, and emotions. It is the place of the expression of your person—your *personality*. It houses your thoughts, your hopes, your dreams, and your fears. Though the physical cannot reach in and physically touch the soul, your soul is nourished by physical affection as well as wounded by physical abuse. A hug can spill over from the physical and warm your soul. A slap can sting your heart as well as your face. Your soul lives in your body. It can *exercise power* over your physical body.

In times of danger, the soul can override the body's physical capacity. There are stories of great feats of strength where will has overcome matter, where the human desire is so great it supersedes physical odds. Examples can be found with athletes or with a parent whose child is in danger. There are also accounts of those who have been paralyzed by fear—physically capable yet frozen by sheer willpower.

The soul can imprint itself on us outwardly. Fear, grief, or anger can etch themselves upon a face after years of expressing physically the inner turmoil of the soul. Likewise, joy, peace, and strength can leave their mark on a face. Fear of rejection can change a person's posture, causing one to cower or stoop, while confidence holds another erect and straight.

Just as your physical body was created by God, so was your soul.

> For you created my inmost being…
>
> —PSALM 139:13

The soul is the inner being. It should be governed by the will, which is governed by your strongest base of influence. It draws information from your mind and considers your physical needs in its analysis of natural information. It draws on past experiences and is forged and molded with each passing day. It can be both analytical and emotional.

The soul is different from the physical body, yet the soul inhabits the body much as a hand fills a glove. The body is lifeless, expressionless, and useless without the soul.

A third dimension is the spirit, which is often described as your *heart*.

> Love the Lord your God with all your heart and with all your soul and with all your mind and with all your strength.
>
> —Mark 12:30

When your life is divinely ordered, your spirit will direct your soul and mind, which in turn will guide your physical self. It is the goal of this book to introduce truths to you that will lead you into a proper restoration of all of these areas. If you are ready for transformation, "then you will know the truth, and the truth will set you free" (John 8:32).

Let's ask God for truth and discernment.

> *Father,*
>
> *In the name of Jesus, I ask that Your truth would light the paths of my inner heart, that I might hear Your still, small voice above the din of any other influence or opinion. Lord, You fashioned and formed me in the secret place of my mother's womb, not for bondage but for liberty. Though I cannot go back to the quiet stillness of the womb, I now ask You to fashion me once again in the secret place of my heart. Create a place of refuge and peace where there has been*

turmoil and torment. It is safe to be honest with You, for You could never hurt me. You have already proven this by dying for me so I might live. With You I will be honest, for I know You are the Truth that sets me free. Amen.

WHAT IS THE TRUTH?

You have just prayed for an encounter with truth—or more specifically, *the Truth*. I now want to give you a frame of reference for this truth. It cannot vary, and it is much higher and far greater than any truth the world has already offered. To obtain this truth, you must move beyond the mere opinions of mankind. You need to pursue truth that is formative and able to re-create, able to bring healing and restoration, and able to carry within itself a seed of life.

God's truth supersedes the authority of any other present "truth" or fleeting cultural trend. These vary and fluctuate with the whims of media and men. Truth must never change, and thus it must be timeless. It must be truth that is ancient, because it existed *before* us and will continue on long *after* us. It must be eternal truth.

Eternal truth cannot be found within the confines or reasoning power of mortal man. As I said earlier in this chapter, the created cannot create. Man can be creative and reproduce. But man cannot initiate creation. No man is supreme in authority. Even if an individual or government could rise to such a level, it would only be for a moment, a tiny speck on the timeline of eternity. No man lives forever.

Eternal truth must be born out of a motive so pure no human can conceive it. It must come from someone superior to humans in every way. It can only come from God:

> "My thoughts are completely different from yours," says the LORD. "And my ways are far beyond anything you could imagine. For just as the heavens are higher than the earth, so are my ways higher than your ways and my thoughts higher than your thoughts."
>
> —Isaiah 55:8–9, NLT

God is making it very clear: He doesn't think like us. Because we are merely the created, we cannot even *imagine* His ways. So expansive is this gap that He uses something we can see—the distance spanned between the heights of heaven and the terrain of earth—to describe it. Can a man standing on this earth reach up and touch the heights of heaven?

No, even from Mount Everest—Earth's highest mountain—this is impossible. There is a great expanse between the way we think, reason, dream, hope, and live and the way God does things. As a matter of fact, He doesn't *do* things—He *embodies* them. We live; He *is* life. We love; He *is* love. We think; He *is* knowledge, wisdom, and understanding. We dream; He *is* the fulfillment of every dream, even ones we are not yet capable of conceiving.

These comparisons are made to explain that from where we are, we can never apprehend or comprehend

His thoughts or ways. Being earthbound, we are bound to time; we think and live relative to time. He is boundless because He lives in the realm of the timeless eternal. We all had a beginning and, most likely, we will have an end.

He has no beginning; He *is* the beginning. He always was and always will be.

This alone is a hard concept for us to grasp because everything we have ever known or experienced had an origin, a beginning. We can grasp the concept of having no end, but having no beginning is a hard concept to comprehend. Though change and new beginnings are fathomable to our human mind, having no beginning and being changeless are not.

Though one nation may conquer and dominate another, elevating one leader above others for a short time, the winds of change will blow. Yet God is the Ruler Supreme over all the nations, the King over every earthly king or kingdom. He outranks any natural or spiritual authority and power. He is the *ultimate authority.*

Every created thing—all creation—is under the authority of God. Therefore, we can safely say that His voice or opinion overrides all others. The cumulative wisdom of all mankind is foolishness to Him.

> For the wisdom of this world is foolishness in God's sight. As it is written: "He catches the wise in their craftiness"; and again, "The Lord knows that the thoughts of the wise are futile."
>
> —1 CORINTHIANS 3:19–20

Only His truth and wisdom bring hope, fruit, and lasting liberty. Man may *know* truth, but God *is* truth.

> Then you will know the truth, and the truth will set you free.
>
> —JOHN 8:32

To know truth is to be intimately acquainted with it. Knowing is more than the mere acknowledgment of its existence. It implies a relationship. *Strong's Exhaustive Concordance* defines the term *know* as found in this scripture as "absolutely; in a great variety of applications and implications; an adherence to truth not only on a mental level thus changing our perceptions on merely a single level, but one which permeates until it reaches every area of our being."[2]

This is what happens when truth becomes a part of you.

You need to know truth with a deeper intimacy and to a greater degree than you've known the lie. You once lived a lie, and it captivated you; *if you live the truth, it will liberate you.*

To *know* truth is to *live* truth. It is the truth you live that sets you free. Then it penetrates deeper and reaches further than the lie, dispelling with its light any darkness lurking in the remote areas of your soul. Knowledge of the truth alone will not be enough. You need a *relationship* with truth. The question changes from "*What* is the truth?" to "*Who* is the Truth?"

I am married, and though others may know about my husband or know him personally on some levels, they will never know him in the same way or dimension I do. They may be acquainted with John Bevere the friend, minister, author, employer, or father. But I alone know him on the intimate, private level of *husband*. That is *our* relationship. Though others may know him by what he does, I know John Bevere by who he is. We are one.

You must become one with the truth because you have been one with the lie. Who is the Truth?

> Jesus answered, "I am the way and the truth and the life."
>
> —JOHN 14:6

He is the way you seek. He is the Truth who sets you free. He offers you the life you long for. You may right now be questioning what I say: "I know Him, but I do not feel free. I feel captive!" He allows captivity to serve as an invitation to experience Him on a deeper level. He is drawing you closer, drawing you deeper, to His side. He wants to be your companion and Lord as you journey from captivity to freedom. He does not want you to try it in your own strength again. You've already tried and failed.

He wants the glory from this escape. All He requires from you is a deeper level of surrender to truth, a yielding of your will to His.

THE DIFFERENCE BETWEEN LIES AND TRUTH

After we accept Christ as the ultimate truth we must realize that the enemy still wishes to deceive us. It is important to recognize a few key principles about lies and truth.

1. *Lies are often easier to embrace than truths.* One lie is easily followed by another and yet another until the truth is found out.

2. *Truth will stop the progression of lies.* When you are constantly bombarded with lies, you begin to believe the lie. Likewise, when you lie to others or to yourself long enough, you are soon deceived and begin to believe the lie and doubt the truth.

3. *Transforming truths are the most costly to embrace.* Although God freely offers these truths to whosoever will embrace them, transforming truth is costly because it requires an admission of your own inability to provide. It is a call to lay aside your pride and surrender to humility and dependence.

When you have spent yourself of your natural strength, resources, talents, and provisions, God invites you to come to Him empty-handed. He does not want your money or labor—He wants your empty life. In exchange for your surrender, He gives you life, an everlasting covenant, and faithful, unwavering love.

But you cannot come to Him in the strength of your own merits. You must strip yourself from the lies and embrace His truth. He is calling you to the river of baptism, where you are totally immersed into life and all that is death is washed away. Such a rebirth is available for every area of your life.

Acknowledge your need for Him, your need for His help. Ask Him to sow a seed of truth into the soil of your humbled heart. Ask yourself:

- *Have I ever trusted someone only to be disappointed by that person?*

- *Have I ever disappointed myself?*

- *Have I ever believed something was true, only to find out later that it was not?*

- *Have I ever lied to someone?*

- *Have I ever lied to myself?*

The seed of truth is first planted in the rich soil of your spirit. Guarded there, it is allowed a safe atmosphere in which to grow. As it grows, you must tend it as you would a natural garden, watering it with the truth of God's Word and uprooting any additional weeds of destruction and deception.

Even words and deeds can be seeds. Some of the seeds that have been planted in your life may have been seeds that produced pain or destruction. Such seeds need to be uprooted. New seeds of truth should be planted—ones that will yield a harvest of healing and strength for your life.

This is a new day, a new season for you. A time to plant new seed and reap a harvest of fresh produce in your life. I know you are ready for change.

This will mean uprooting old plantings and reconditioning the soil to create an atmosphere for the new. God is the ultimate gardener. He takes the soil of a fearful, hardened heart, removes the weeds, amends the soil, plants new seeds, and waters them with His Word.

Are you ready to allow the Master Gardener to transform you? If so, pray this prayer:

> *Heavenly Father,*
>
> *You said that I could come to You with nothing but my failures and You would give me water that would quench this thirsting in my soul. You invited me to dine on the Bread of Life and to partake of milk and wine. I have tried to satisfy myself with bread, and it failed me. I have tried to comfort myself with milk and console myself with wine, and they failed me.*
>
> *Yet, You speak of water, bread, wine, and milk I cannot provide. They are only found in You. Forgive me for my foolish efforts to satisfy myself with natural things. They do not fill me; they only temporarily postpone my real longing—which is for You. Lord, let me be as the woman at the well; give me living water. I humble myself*

and confess my need and utter dependence on You. Lead me in Your paths, and I will walk in them. I don't want to walk alone in this bondage any longer; I invite You into every area of my life where falsehood has prevailed. Transform me! In Jesus' name, amen.

Chapter 4

THE IMAGE OF THE LIE

No matter how plain a woman may be, if truth and honesty are written across her face, she will be beautiful.[1]

—ELEANOR ROOSEVELT

It is not what he has, or even what he does which expresses the worth of a man, but what he is.[2]

—HENRI-FRÉDÉRIC AMIEL

If Jesus is the express image of the truth, then what is the express image of the lie? Just as truth needs an image for expression, power, and validation, so the lie must have an image or it remains powerless.

You and I are painfully and constantly made aware of the image of the lie. It is everywhere we even happen to glance. It is projected on television and at the movies, plastered on billboards, and splashed across magazine covers. Most of us encounter it daily on one level or another.

Today's expression of this image has been built by multitudes of advertising and media experts who feed off our external influences. On the surface there is nothing wrong with this image; it is what she represents that is dangerous. She is the image of an ideal woman.

Portrayals of the ideal woman are presented to all ethnic groups. She never ages, and behind her facade of perfection she mocks every flaw and imperfection of others. Her skin is flawless in tone and complexion. Her nose is straight—not too small or too large. Her eyes are bright and lack any dark shadows, circles, or lines around them. They are encased in luminous, wrinkle-free skin. Her lips are full and artfully shaped. Her teeth are perfect and gleaming white.

Her body is perfectly proportioned and sits atop long, strong legs. She is the perfect height! Her breasts never age (or nurse)! This image is always just beyond our reach, taunting us with her seductive eyes. Who is she anyway?

Her name doesn't really matter; she is not real. She is an image molded and forged by the spirit of this world. She is a Photoshopped, deaf, dumb, and blind idol.

Though we know she is not real, women of all ages look at her in awe. The younger are inspired and the older are depressed.

Men are not immune to these comparisons, for this woman has a counterpart. He is naturally gifted with a great body and sense of style. He always has the right words to say, whatever the situation. He never loses his eight-pack or his hair.

This man works a full day at the office, then returns home ready to repair all things mechanical or electronic with ease. His unparalleled intelligence is evidenced by the row of degrees hanging on his wall. He maintains the perfect balance of toughness and tenderness at all times. The dividends of his portfolio provide him with abundant financial stability not only for himself but also for his wife or girlfriend. He is the fastest, strongest, and best at every sport, and he enjoys all manner of cultural activities.

This image too eludes attainment, disapproving others with his steely gaze. Yet he also is deaf and dumb, an idol.

IDOLS

Before I go further it is important to describe the worship of idols or idolatry in contemporary terms. For until I do so, idolatry still may seem a foreign term. *An idol is anything you draw your strength from or give your strength to.* It is how you spend yourself—your time, your efforts, your thoughts. It is the driving force behind your actions. It is what makes you feel confident and comfortable. *Nelson's Illustrated Bible Dictionary* defines an idol as "something we ourselves make into a god."[3] It can be anything that stands between you and God—a substitute for God.

How can people you have never met influence you so profoundly? Because you have not allowed the imprint of God to influence you as deeply as they have influenced you. Without a definitive raising of *His* standard, you are likely to accept the seductive, graven image of the world.

> The fashioners of an image—all of them are emptiness, and the things they delight in cannot profit.
>
> —ISAIAH 44:9, RHM

To *fashion* something is to make, model, form, or manufacture. In the Bible the words *image* and *idol* are used interchangeably with the exception of two references. Therefore we could go into the above scripture and bring it forward into today's terms. Then it would read:

> The ones who make and model idols or fashion images—all of them are empty and lifeless. What they value and prize *cannot* profit or help you.
>
> —AUTHOR'S PARAPHRASE

Isaiah tells us in the second part of this verse why this is so: "For their idols neither see nor know. No wonder those who worship them are so ashamed" (TLB). The ancient idols or graven images were forged by craftsmen who made them out of wood or stone. Sometimes they were overlaid with precious metals or costly jewels. But they were never more than lifeless—dead—wood or stone.

No matter how dressed up they were on the outside, they had no life on the inside.

The people would model and form images and idols and then bow down to what they themselves had crafted. These crafted images (of wood, stone, or precious metals) were made by the created (humans). Then the created subjected themselves to the crafted. Crying out to images without breath, those with eyes asked guidance of blind idols. Those with breath, mouth, and voice cried out to mute idols with lifeless lips. Those with ears to hear cried out to deaf ears of stone. They offered fragrant incense and food to idols who could neither smell nor taste.

The created longed to worship the work of their own hands, though these idols could never raise a finger in response. The created cannot *create*—it can only *craft*. The crafted cannot even craft.

You might be thinking, *But, Lisa, I've never bowed my knees to an idol or sought wisdom from a graven image. So what does this have to do with me?*

When you don't take your problems to God, you end up crying out to the very problem that has you ensnared. When you worship the work of your hands or the works of the flesh, you are worshiping images of the *creation* and not the *Creator*. Let's go into the New Testament to find how this could be relevant today:

> For although they knew God, they neither glorified him as God nor gave thanks to him, but their

thinking became futile and their foolish hearts
were darkened.

—ROMANS 1:21

They knew there was a Creator God, but they did not
want to glorify Him or acknowledge His provision by
thanking Him. They turned their eyes from God and
began to worship images. Soon their hearts became like
the idols they worshiped—void of light and futile. This
parallels Isaiah's description of useless idols.

*The image you behold is the image you become—not out-
wardly but inwardly.* The apostle Paul further expanded
this concept in the Book of Romans:

> Although they claimed to be wise, they became
> fools and exchanged the glory of the immortal God
> for images made to look like mortal man and birds
> and animals and reptiles.
>
> —ROMANS 1:22–23

The idol worshipers claimed to be wise creators, but
when you bow to that which is equal to (mere man) or
lower than yourself, you become degraded, abased, and
deceived. When you serve what is lifeless you die.

> Therefore God gave them over in the sinful desires
> of their hearts to sexual impurity for the degrading
> of their bodies with one another. *They exchanged the
> truth of God for a lie*, and worshiped and served

created things rather than the Creator—who is forever praised. Amen.

—Romans 1:24–25,
emphasis added

They wanted to serve the works of their flesh, so God
let them become mastered by their flesh. They worshiped
images fashioned after their own desires, so God turned
them over to their basest desires.

Where there is idol or image worship, sexual sin can
always be found. It comes in the form of promiscuity
and perversion. Sexual impurity is accompanied by an
increased prominence of sexual expression. Nudity is
common. What once was saved for intimacy is now displayed for all to view. Men and women who were inwardly
fashioned for the habitation of the Spirit of God become
temples of sexual perversion and depravity instead.

Sexual perversion and promiscuity are not merely physical acts. There is a much deeper and stronger spiritual con-
nection that ties the physical sexual realm to the unseen
spiritual realm.

*We exchange the truth for a lie whenever we worship or
serve the created and not the Creator.*

We all serve something or someone. It's not an option.
So the question is not *if* you serve but *whom* you serve.
As Christians it is important to determine whether we are
serving an image of God or God Himself.

If you are serving the gods or idols of this world you
will recognize it in your desire to conform to the world's
image. You will want the acceptance and approval of your

culture. You will desire what the culture desires. You will seek its reward and system of social and financial security. The image will always be before you, inviting and enticing you to be like it. You will look toward it, gauging your success or failures according to the messages you receive from these idols.

If you serve God and not merely an image from any other source, you will experience a constant and ongoing transformation into His image. *All lasting liberation, healing, or change begins with inward transformation.*

There are multitudes of books offering outwardly focused information—diet plans, exercise regimens, self-improvement suggestions for your makeup or wardrobe. This book is not one of them. I'm writing to tell you that only what God does in your life will last. Time is short, and this message is urgent. *God is calling you to radical transformation.*

Perhaps this chapter has opened your eyes to the reality of who you've been serving. Your situation may not have anything to do with an eating disorder, but you've come to realize that, in some way, instead of allowing yourself to be transformed into *God's* image, you've been trying to conform *God* to *your* image. As a result, your image of God is distorted. In reality it is the image of *you*. It's an idol.

It's time to stop conforming and start transforming. You've known the lie, but now you've been introduced to the truth. Now is the time to be honest. What image are you serving?

JUDGING OR MISJUDGING?

Because we have judged by appearances, we often misjudge. Adornment is like a bowl that holds fruit, one that could be displayed on the dining room table. It is beautifully crafted and forged of cut crystal, yet holds in its beauty fruit that is artificial and tasteless. The fruit may look initially inviting because it is surrounded by outward beauty, but if handled or sampled, the fruit will soon be revealed as worthless.

Meanwhile, somewhere in the pantry there is a worn and tattered crate that holds real produce. It is not beautiful, yet it bears what is delicious, fresh, and life-giving. If you were hungry—hungry for truth, hungry for what is real—you'd turn from the beauty of the cut crystal bowl filled with artificial fruit and head for the useful, fruitful crate.

God judges us by our *fruit*, not our *fruit bowls*. He wants our inner adornment to be fresh and useful, not cold and beautiful yet artificial. Therefore, we are mistaken when we judge others by the packaging of outward appearances.

If you want the true transformation I've been writing about to begin in your life, it starts by crying out to God and asking Him to reveal Himself to you (and as a result, worshiping Him). Ask yourself these questions:

    ॐ *Do I long to fit the image of an ideal woman or man?*

- *Do I strive to meet the shape, size, success, or social standing of celebrities and icons?*

- *Do I believe that these ideals will bring me love and happiness?*

- *Have my prayers been answered through my worship of these idols?*

- *Do I believe being seductive makes me desirable?*

- *Do I trade sexual desirability for my purity?*

- *Am I afraid God is not strong enough to transform me?*

- *Am I ready to forgive myself for focusing on the idols and images of the world?*

- *Am I ready to repent for reducing God's image to that of my own understanding, reasoning, knowledge, ability, or experience?*

The next step is to repent for allowing other things to block or distort your image of God. By doing this you renounce the hold and influence of the idols in your life. This will be an act of submission to God and aggression against a long-term spiritual stronghold in our culture. I've written this prayer to help you, but please feel free to mix your own words with the words printed on this page.

Father,

I come before You in the name of Jesus, in the name of truth. Lord, I repent of looking to the graven images and idols of this world when I should have come to You for my strength. I renounce their hold and influence in my life. I cast their impressions from my mind and their illusions from before my eyes. Father, remove the veil from my eyes. I want to see You and You alone. Let Your image outshine any other in my life. Imprint Your truth deeper within me than any of the lies of the false god of this age. I turn from the image of the lie toward the knowledge of Your Son. Reveal Yourself to me in a deeper and very real way. I give You permission to invade this private and personal area of my life. In Jesus's name, amen.

Chapter 5

SELF-IMAGE OR SELF-WORSHIP?

This is true humility: not thinking less of
ourselves but thinking of ourselves less.[1]

—RICK WARREN

B Y PRAYING YOUR version of the prayer at the end of the last chapter, the power of God's Spirit is there with you now to rescue you from the images and lies that have held you captive. Having renounced any tendency toward the image of the world, it is now time to go a step further and renounce another prevalent image.

This image is much more subtle and widely accepted in most religious circles, though it is not found on any list in the kingdom. It actually is a religious idea, one of the very first to be introduced. Yet there is a problem with religious ideas and traditions; they are powerless to liberate you.

The religious people of Jesus's day had turned away from the living commands of God to conform to the wisdom and traditions of man—an example of turning from the Creator toward the created. Jesus explained that in so doing, they nullified—negated or canceled out—the very power they needed. They had exchanged the truth for a lie, life for death, and power for impotence.

> You have let go of the commands of God and are holding on to the traditions of men…setting aside the commands of God in order to observe your own traditions! Thus you nullify the word of God by your tradition that you have handed down.
>
> —MARK 7:8–9, 13

Power is not found in principles but hidden within the Word of God. We need the *Word* of God, for hidden in its manifold truths is the *power* of God. Though the word of man may contain form and structure, without the life and power of God it is useless. It cannot transform our hearts, though it may please our minds. We need substance and relationship. To apprehend this we must strip away the veil of self-worship.

You may immediately reject this, arguing, "How could I worship myself? I feel bad about myself. I have a bad self-image!"

To this objection I would counter, "Whenever you are limited to your self-image, then your *image of self* becomes your master."

I want to challenge some typical deceptions. Here is one: *If only I could feel good about myself, then I would be fulfilled.*

God does not want us fulfilled through the avenue of self. He wants us fulfilled through Him. The Word of God is not set up to cause us to feel *good* about *ourselves*. It is set up to reveal to us a *good God*. To *feel* good about ourselves, we would have to *be* good. But even Jesus would not assign the adjective of *good* to Himself.

> "Why do you call me good?" Jesus answered. "No one is good—except God alone."
>
> —MARK 10:18; cf. LUKE 18:19

Jesus did not say, "Wow, I really feel really good about Myself. I am good, and you can be good, too! Just follow Me!" No, He wasn't looking to be labeled as "good" by human standards; His goal was to glorify His heavenly Father, who is the very essence of goodness.

Though Jesus was the Son of God, He did not grasp at equality with God the Father by calling Himself good. God alone is good, and through His goodness we are restored and He is glorified.

When my youngest son was three years old, he liked to hold my face between his two soft hands and look at me face-to-face. He wanted me up close in order to know he had my full attention and affection. He looked me intently in the eyes until I returned his gaze; then he kissed me. He needed the closeness. In it, he was not aware of himself—he was only aware of the two of us.

It's the same with God. He wants you to be so totally aware of your relationship with Him that you lose consciousness of what is around you. He doesn't want to draw you close to see your flaws; He wants to hold you close to captivate you with His love.

WHEN DID IT BEGIN?

You began life with this same unawareness of self, but when did it leave? Awareness of self is not something you are born with; it is forged through *pain*, *pressure*, and *praise*.

- Pain causes you to become aware of something that you previously were not aware of.

- Pressure brings hidden talents or flaws to the surface.

- Praise tests what you are made of and points out talents or assets.

Somewhere between childhood and adulthood we lose our bearings. Whether we intend to or not, we exchange the truth for a lie. This usually happens progressively as we are exposed to the opinions of others and allow those opinions to influence us more than the opinions of God. We begin to believe we are what we do, what we have, what we wear, what we know, how we look, or who we know.

For each of us it happens in different measures and at various times. Wherever there is diversity or difference we find comparison and criticism. For me, captivity began during puberty. Most of us remember the agony we endured at various stages during this period of life. This was when I remember being most body conscious. I felt as though my body had betrayed me.

I was a very late bloomer, and I decided I didn't want to bloom at all. I came to this conclusion after hearing from my peers who had gone before me, and from various health movies, what I would have to endure. I did not want bra straps for boys to snap. I had no desire to shave my legs and underarms. The very thought of bleeding and cramping monthly sounded like a horrible intrusion on my favorite sport, swimming.

Each girl was assessed according to her physical development. Boys noticed the girls who were developing quickly. For me the word *flat* took on a totally new meaning. I was beginning to feel a further separation between the *physical* me and the *real* me, the *obvious* and the *unseen*.

Self-image is a defense mechanism. It is the image you project while you try to protect who you really are. It's the *projected* image versus the *protected* one, the one left vulnerable when you lose the innocence of what I call "self-unawareness." In a moment's time, I had lost the unconscious sense of my physical body. In that instant, I was tethered to the awkward and uncomfortable.

The world believes the opposite of being self-conscious is having a "good" self-image or self-esteem. But I believe we are called to something higher. I believe that the opposite of conscious is unconscious. Therefore, opposite of self-consciousness should be self-*un*consciousness. Losing consciousness of self happens when you become more conscious or aware of God and His will than you are of yourself and your will. This is a work of the Spirit, accomplished progressively as you renounce your natural limitations and abandon yourself to Him.

- *When you think of being tethered to or measured by something other than God, what incident (positive or negative) comes first to your mind?*

- *How old were you?*

- *Describe yourself before this incident—how you viewed yourself and how you felt.*

- *Describe your immediate reaction to this incident, if you remember it.*

- *In what areas are you still self-conscious?*

> ᴓ *Would you like to be untied from these images,*
> *whether they are good or bad? To no longer be*
> *limited to self's perception?*

Let's pray and sever those ties:

> *Dear Father,*
> *I want to be free like a child again. Untie me*
> *from self and bind me to You. I don't want to be*
> *alone and aware of me; I long to be aware of us.*
> *I turn my eyes from the image of self and direct*
> *them toward Your face. Draw me close, that I*
> *might behold You and be held by You. I tear*
> *down the idol of self and build the altar of God.*
> *In Jesus's name, amen.*

THE ROOT OF THE LIE

So far in this chapter, I've discussed the personal, or soulish, root of self-image or self-consciousness; now I want to dig deeper and go down to the very origin of *self*. Where did this consciousness all begin?

We find the first awareness of self in Genesis, the book of beginnings. In Genesis 2:25, Adam and Eve were both *naked* and *unashamed*. They were undressed and unaware of their nakedness. They were conscious only of the perfect union that existed between them—separate, yet one; individual, yet complementary; different, yet similar. It was an awareness so intense and complete that it overshadowed their physical selves.

The Bible offers no description of their stature, skin, or hair coloring. I'm so glad! If we had a description of how they looked, we would make that the "ideal." The Bible doesn't even give their ages at this introduction. We have no idea whether Adam and Eve were thin or fat, tall or short, black or white. I am sure they embodied and exemplified pure physical perfection—the perfection of the origin of the species of human life in a time before disease, sickness, and death.

Shame had yet to creep between them. It did not exist in this garden of creation. Not only were they naked before each other, but also both were completely uncovered in the presence of their Creator. They were free in His presence and in the presence of each other. God and Adam rejoiced freely in the glorious dawn of God's last living creation: woman.

This innocent beginning was conceived in a perfect environment, an atmosphere of perfect unity with each other and their Creator. Their awareness encompassed three areas: the Creator; the creation that flourished, sheltered, and provided for them; and one another. We cannot be sure how long this time of innocence endured.

But all too soon their innocence was lost forever. They were made aware of themselves. This self-awareness came with an awareness of distinct inequality with God. And thus they were about to be tempted with the knowledge of good:

> "You will not surely die," the serpent said to the woman. "For God knows that when you eat of it *your eyes will be opened*, and you will be like God, knowing good and evil."
>
> —GENESIS 3:4–5,
> *emphasis added*

Adam and Eve were presented with the ultimate temptation, that of ultimate perfection: *to be like God*, to have eyes opened to the way things really are, to pass from the dependency of children and know good from evil without any involvement of authority, to be lord of self. It was an appealing proposition. The serpent promised them an opening of their eyes, implying they were blinded to some part of the big picture. Could something they needed have been obscured from their present level of vision?

They'd never known or experienced evil. It is also quite possible that they hadn't even known good. *They'd only known God.*

The knowledge of good and evil is the law of sin and death. God wanted Adam to remain free in the liberty of his knowledge of God. Adam had gained this knowledge, or relationship, by walking with God. His relationship with God was not based on rules; it was grounded in love. Adam did not need the knowledge of good and evil to walk with God; he already walked with Him. Satan did not want Adam and Eve to remain free and alive under the law of liberty, so he perverted God's protective warning.

Adam and Eve listened to Satan's lie and exchanged their pure knowledge of God for the knowledge of good and evil.

In that moment their thoughts and ways became completely different from God's. He is never selfish or self-serving; He is Father in the purest and truest sense of the word.

Adam and Eve had experienced God on an intensively intimate and pure level. He'd formed them lovingly with His hand and quickened them with His very breath. In foolish rebellion they turned from the Creator and chose to embrace the created.

The fruit of the forbidden tree looked good and pleasant. It could impart wisdom. This sounds like our description of an idol, doesn't it? As Eve reached for the *fruit* of creation, she turned her back on the *God* of creation. As Adam took the fruit from the hand of his wife, he dropped the hand that forged him.

> Then the *eyes of both of them were opened*, and they realized they were naked.
>
> —Genesis 3:7,
> *emphasis added*

Adam's and Eve's eyes were opened; for the first time they perceived their nakedness. The Bible does not say that their clothes fell off and then they realized they were naked; it says that their *eyes were opened*. The veil or covering had not been around their *bodies*; it had been over their eyes.

Now they saw into a dimension previously shrouded from their view. Stripped of the eternal veil of light, they beheld the dark and earthly dimension. The veil of light that had cloaked their eyes was replaced by one that draped their hearts. This shrouding of the heart created a habitation for darkness.

The couple's transgression was accompanied by a heightened consciousness of self. Sin gave birth to shame. Innocence and purity were replaced with knowledge and sensuality. This new sight required a veiling of their bodies. The first thing they did was cover themselves. Sin always requires a covering.

Sin opened their eyes to the visible and closed them to the invisible. They gained sight of reality and lost sight of eternity. Fear dimmed their new sight, for the light within had turned to darkness.

Before their transgression, their eyes had been good and their beings flooded with light. They had seen only light. In the presence of God there is only light—there was no shadow about Him. Light dispels darkness. But living now in the temporal, they knew both good and evil. Now their eyes beheld darkness.

The darkness brought with it fear and foolishness. In fear, man and woman retreated into deeper darkness in the shadows of the trees. Darkness will always flee from the presence of light.

> Then the man and his wife heard the sound of the Lord God as he was walking in the garden in the cool of the day, and they hid from the Lord God among the trees of the garden.
> —Genesis 3:8

They thought they could hide from God. They did not want their deeds to be brought to the light, so they withdrew into the shadows of creation instead of falling at the feet of their Creator.

If you believe lies, you become afraid of truth. Turning from truth to a lie causes the light in you to become darkness. You lose sight of the eternal and become limited to the obvious. So then how do you eradicate a lie? To eradicate a lie you must go back to the truths that existed before the lie.

It is imperative that truth is fixed and established in your life. *Eternal truths produce eternal results; temporary truths produce temporary results.*

I find it amazing that we do not find physical descriptions of any individuals until *after* Adam and Eve left the garden. Only then were men and women defined by age, children, labor, and accomplishments. Occasionally we find a person described in terms of his relationship with God. But these are isolated instances and always set apart from the rest. The lives of such people are highlighted uniquely in the unfolding plan of God for mankind.

Interspersed throughout the rest of the Old Testament, we find physical descriptions of many leaders: Sarah, Rebekah, Rachel, Leah, Joseph, David, Goliath, Absalom, Solomon, and Elisha to name a few. In the New Testament we find a description of John the Baptist, describing his clothing and appearance. After the description of John, it would appear that the need for physical descriptions became less important. The emphasis switches from the *outward and natural appearance* to the *hidden and eternal person*. From the obvious to the unseen. Why? Because Jesus came to rescue what had been lost in the garden.

Paul describes it this way:

> Therefore, from now on, we regard no one according to the flesh. Even though we have known Christ according to the flesh, yet now we know Him thus no longer. Therefore, if anyone is in Christ, he is a new creation; old things have passed away; behold, all things have become new.
>
> —2 Corinthians 5:16–17, NKJV

As a believer you are to change the way you evaluate or view things. No longer are you to know or understand people according to what you see in the natural dimension of the flesh. Paul uses the transition of the knowledge of Jesus to explain this. At one time, Jesus walked among His disciples and other believers on this earth as the Son of Man. But now He is in heaven, and it is impossible to know Him according to natural terms. You now learn of Him by the Spirit, through the Scriptures. He is progressively revealed not as the Son of Man but as the Son of God.

Jesus's disciples had known Him as the natural man; now He was revealed as the eternal. Paul admonished the believers to adopt this same view of each other—to look beyond the earthly and obvious to glimpse the eternal, "Christ in [us], the hope of glory" (Colossians 1:27).

When you turn to Christ, the shroud of death is stripped away; once again you can glimpse the eternal. It is a process involving the retraining of your mind and will. Instead of serving self you must now subject and submit self once again to the Creator. To lose an awareness of self you must gain an awareness of God.

I am not talking about a total loss of consciousness where you no longer care for your physical self. I am talking about escaping the realm or dimension in which self becomes your master.

If you desire to gain a greater awareness of God, then pray this prayer:

> *Dear heavenly Father,*
>
> *Please forgive any tendency I have toward the worship of self. You said that I was to take up my cross, deny myself, and follow You. Lord, for too long I have not denied myself; I have been overwhelmingly conscious of myself. I have lived to protect and provide for myself. Please forgive me. I renounce the fallen nature that would seek to serve self, and I ask You to teach me to serve You. I want to become increasingly conscious of Your will and ways and less and less conscious of my own will and ways. Restore my sight. Let me glimpse again the eternal and lose sight of the sensual and earthbound. I avert my eyes from myself and turn them toward You. In Jesus's name, amen.*

Chapter 6

THE IDOL TUMBLES

We know what we are, but know not what we may be.[1]

—William Shakespeare

Now I WANT to tell you the rest of my story, how God delivered me from my idol. My summer back home in Indiana proved to be very different from all the other summer breaks I'd had. That summer I heard the gospel for the first time, and I became a Christian. It filled a void in me that I had tried to fill with attention from boys. I began to relax. God loved me just the way I was. For a time the voice was silent, and I stopped my excessive exercising, dieting, and drinking; I began to look healthy and relaxed again.

Christians love to eat. Every social event I attended was centered on food! At church picnics we ate; after church we ate; on dates we ate. I now had a new problem—my excessive tendency to drink had transferred to a consumption of food. I felt permission to eat, but I'd never faced my excessive tendencies until now.

Around Christian tables no one talked about calories or the vices of food. Food was a celebration. I celebrated with them, and before long I had put back on most of the weight I had lost.

It was during this time that I met John. At the end of the school year, we got engaged, and I needed to return home to Indiana to prepare for the wedding. I was a little overweight, but John didn't seem to notice.

By August my weight had floated back up—and it was no longer muscle. I was totally out of shape, and the weight was clinging to my stomach, hips, and thighs. I had only two months before my wedding. I decided to exercise and get back in shape while I was home.

But home was filled with turmoil, and I responded to this turmoil by eating. If I was bored, I would walk over to the refrigerator, open the door, and look in even though I wasn't hungry.

My days revolved around weighing myself, eating breakfast, weighing myself, running errands, eating lunch, weighing myself, making phone calls for wedding arrangements, eating dinner, and weighing myself again. I became more and more discouraged—so I binged more and more!

As I binged I assured myself it was all right to eat everything I wanted *today*, because *tomorrow* I would not eat at all! Then I would eat until it was painful, knowing the next day I would starve myself.

I would toss restlessly, experiencing nightmares in which I ate everything in the refrigerator. I would wake in a sweat and reassure myself that I had not done what I dreamed! Other nights I wrestled dark fears so real that I felt as though I wore them like a weight on my chest.

The next day would come, and although I'd determined not to eat at all, my mind was consumed with thoughts of food—how good whatever I saw would taste. I would open and close the refrigerator and freezer just to look. I would weigh myself first thing in the morning and again in the afternoon and evening. Often I had not even lost a pound! After an entire day of not eating, the needle on the scale would not budge off the same weight I'd been for days. Discouraged, I would binge again.

I tried liquid diets and high-protein diets, but they failed.

I missed John. My parents were separated. All my friends were out of town. I was alone, and I felt fat and ugly.

Then came the day of reckoning. With only four weeks left until my wedding, I needed to rent a slip for my wedding gown. I brought my dress to the store with me so we could determine the appropriate slip style and length. My wedding gown buttoned almost entirely down the back. I stepped into it and pushed the sides together so the saleswoman could button it.

"Honey, something is wrong," she said as she shook her head.

"What do you mean?" I questioned.

"This must not be your gown. There is no way you fit into this dress! The buttons are this far apart!" She showed me the distance with her with her finger and thumb. It spanned three or four inches.

I was certain she was mistaken, "Here, it may be a little tight, but I'll push it in." I sucked my stomach in and pinched my waist with my hands.

"Sweetheart, there has been a terrible mistake; this cannot be your gown. I still can't close it; the buttons will tear off if I try."

I could feel my face flushing with frustration and embarrassment.

"Just get me the slip, and I'll try it on without buttoning the dress," I huffed.

"Okay." She walked out, shaking her head doubtfully.

Surely she was exaggerating! While she was gone, I whirled around, contorting myself in order to see the back of my gown. To my horror, she was right. It was impossible even to make the sides meet, let alone button the buttons. I'd outgrown my wedding gown in just the short time since August!

I hurriedly placed my order for the slip, gathered my gown, and raced home. The gown had been a little tight when I bought it. I had been certain I would lose weight at home—not gain it as I had. I never dreamed I would do this! My parents had spent a lot of money on this gown. Now I wondered if I'd ever wear it.

When I arrived home, I ran straight upstairs to my room. After hanging my dress in the closet, I grabbed my Bible and threw myself down on the hardwood floor. I didn't want the comfort of my bed. I wanted the reality of my dilemma to settle in. I cried until I wept, then I wept until I'd spent myself.

"God, how could You allow this to happen? I don't eat all day, and still I can't lose a pound. If I eat only an apple and a yogurt, I gain a pound. I binge and gain two pounds overnight! I'm tired of trying and failing. Why can't I eat like a normal person?"

I thought of my father's and mother's faces when I told them the news of my dress. I felt overwhelmed and very sorry for myself. When the crying was over, a quiet settled over me. It was then I heard a still, small voice.

"Lisa, your weight is an idol to you."

An idol! All I could envision was the picture of a golden calf I had seen in a children's illustrated Bible. I remained quiet and listened.

"When you are lonely, you eat. When you are angry, you eat. When you are bored, you eat. When you are depressed, you eat. When you are happy, you eat."

That about covered it. The voice continued: "You do not come to Me. You do not read My Word. You eat because it is easier."

Every time I did try to read my Bible, the spiritual oppression that I felt in our house was so strong I would fall asleep; yet I could watch TV for hours and remain wide awake. The same thing happened when I tried to pray.

The still, small voice continued, "You feel good about yourself when you are thin and bad about yourself when you are not. You are not Spirit-led; your weight controls your moods and your life. It is an idol to you."

I saw it. It was all true. Weight dominated my thought life and tormented my rest. I had not even shared my faith with friends for fear I'd be rejected because I was overweight. The tears flowed again, but this time they were tears of repentance.

I saw how I'd drawn strength from my weight and not from God. I measured myself by the scales. I was worthy of love if I was thin, but I was not worthy if I was fat.

Once again the voice spoke: "If you'll repent, I will heal your metabolism. Do not diet, and do not weigh yourself. Separate yourself and fast for three days on juices and water, and I will rid your body of its cravings. I will teach you how to eat again. Write down the weight you should be, and put it in your Bible."

I no longer had any idea what my weight should be. My

mind flashed with figures from the many weight charts I'd seen in *Self, Fit, InStyle, Glamour, Bazaar, Shape*, and diet books. Then another thought hit me. "God, You made me. What should I weigh?"

I realized my perceptions were so warped that I would pick a weight far too light for my tall but slender frame. I got very quiet and listened again for the still, small voice. A figure floated into my head; I scribbled the number down and hid it in my Bible. It was more than my former anorexic one hundred three pounds. I initially thought one hundred ten pounds would be nice, but I wrote down another figure.

I got up from the floor, grabbed the scales, and climbed atop my bedroom chair to place them in the attic access in my bedroom closet. God had told me not to weigh myself. I would have to climb up there to get the scales, knowing all the while that I was deliberately disobeying God.

I went into my bathroom and splashed the tears from my face. I headed straight for the grocery store. I walked down the juice aisle, sensing so strongly that God was leading me to buy two quarts of unfiltered organic apple-strawberry juice and a couple gallons of purified water. I had never had unfiltered juice before. The next day would begin a new way of life for me. *I was not fasting to lose weight; I was fasting to fellowship with God.*

My focus during this fast was not weight loss or food. I focused on God and sensed His presence and leading in this action. I sensed that He was pleased with me for repenting and choosing to fast and draw closer to Him.

For the next three days, I drank apple-strawberry juice, straight or diluted, along with purified water. God sustained me in the fast to which He had called me. I went for walks and talked with Him. I listened to praise and worship tapes and wept in His presence.

Then the fast of food was over. Now it was time for me to learn a new lifestyle. I would eat until I was satisfied, not until I was engorged. Because I had never known the difference, praying before eating took on a whole new meaning for me. At mealtime I offered up my food with thanksgiving. I thanked God that food was not my enemy, nor was it my satisfaction. It would bring strength to my body, and in turn, I would worship God.

Fearful thoughts would try to attack me: "If you eat that food you'll get fat! Starve yourself." Gluttony would try to entice me: "That tasted good; you need to eat more!"

I was determined not to eat because it tasted good but because I was feeding myself. I refused to be mastered by my passions any longer. Inwardly I would listen and know when I was satisfied. Then I would put my fork down, not eating another bite.

I was so excited that God was developing this sensitivity in me; I never wanted to disobey it. Even when my family and friends encouraged me to eat more, I would just say, "No, thank you; I am satisfied!"

I felt great! I would walk a mile each night and pray and talk to God. I would not run to burn calories; instead I just walked and talked to God. It brought rest to me. I knew I was losing weight, but I decided not to even notice it.

Three weeks had passed, and my wedding was just a few days away. I had no idea how much I weighed, nor was I even interested. I did need to know that my dress would fit, so I tried it on. Not only did it fit—it hung a little loose! I laughed with joy! I would be able to wear my dress!

My wedding was wonderful, and when I came home to change into my going-away outfit, God stopped me. "Now you can weigh yourself."

I got the scales down and stepped on them. I jumped off the scale and grabbed my Bible. Flipping through it, I found the small slip of paper with the scrawled number. I had forgotten the number I had written down four weeks earlier. I opened up the paper. I jumped back on the scales in disbelief; it was my exact weight! I knew that God had healed my body. He had formed me in my mother's womb. He could heal me.

No longer was I interested in pleasing everyone else; I wanted to please God. He knows what we need even before we ask. He assures us we are fearfully and wonderfully made. He does not measure us by the seen but by the unseen. The following scripture took on a whole new meaning to me.

> Therefore I tell you, do not worry about your life, what you will eat or drink; or about your body, what you will wear. Is not life more important than food, and the body more important than clothes?
>
> —MATTHEW 6:25

Thinking about these things is a waste of time! Jesus admonishes that worrying can't add even an inch to someone's stature. He called the addition of an inch a simple thing. He said if you can't change the small and simple, it is useless to worry about the big.

When fear and worry still tried to torment me with negative thoughts—"What is going to happen when you have children? What if you can't lose the weight?"—I fought back with the Word, not my own experiences. I would counter that God would perfect that which concerned me and that children were a blessing of the Lord. I refused to believe having children would destroy me physically.

Since that time I have had four children and am now experiencing the joy of having grandchildren; throughout it all I have found God faithful to my figure. I relaxed through each pregnancy, nursed each baby, and enjoyed them without worrying about exercising my way to any particular size.

Over the years God has been faithful to keep me at a healthy weight independent of diet and exercise. I have trusted Him to watch over my weight as long as I keep food in the proper place. I eat until I am satisfied. When I am home, I eat healthy because I want to take care of myself, not for weight loss. When it is time to celebrate, I enjoy food. But I eat to celebrate—not to celebrate eating.

In sharing my story, I've talked about reordering disorder and tumbling idols. My hope is that you now realize these steps aren't about losing weight—or overcoming anger, fear, addiction, people pleasing, or any other struggle you're dealing with—they're about recognizing what you've placed your trust in. They are about realizing how you spend yourself. Ask yourself these questions:

- *Do I use something other than God—such as food, accomplishments, or possessions—to meet the needs that only God can meet? What are those needs?*

- *Have those needs truly been met, or am I still dissatisfied?*

- *Have I allowed these false providers to become idols in my life?*

- *Does the measure of these standards—such as my weight, social status, or salary—dictate my mood?*

- *Does my self-esteem heighten when I'm doing well?*

- *Does my self-esteem worsen when my standing suffers?*

- *What have I allowed to control me?*

When I realized the disorder I had created by misplacing my trust and spending all my efforts on the wrong things, I humbled myself with fasting and prayer, and God healed me. In the next chapter, I will share about the power of prayer and fasting to sharpen our spiritual sight.

Chapter 7

SHARPENING YOUR SPIRITUAL SIGHT

Vision is the art of seeing what is invisible to others.[1]
—Jonathan Swift

The Bible says God shares insights and secrets with those who fear Him (Ps. 25:14). Since this book is all about changing your focus from what you look like to what you see, it is only fitting that I discuss the ways you can sharpen your spiritual sight. Prayer and fasting are important ways to do this.

You may or may not be in a position to fast food. In fact, if you are taking medications of any kind (or you have been struggling with any symptoms of an eating disorder, which you can find listed at the end of this book), I strongly advise you *not* to make any changes to your eating habits without consulting a health-care professional. However, even if you are unable to fast *food*, everyone is in a position to fast *something*. It may be TV, social media, magazines, sports, shopping, or a hobby. All of us have areas in which we hide ourselves or waste time. I challenge you to go before our Father and ask Him, by the power of the Holy Spirit, to expose any areas that could be fasted.

Every believer should fast periodically. It is an act of separation to our Father. If you're struggling with your weight, body image, an eating disorder, materialism, or insecurity, you need to fast all the images that have driven you to such abuse or deception.

Jesus gave us invaluable insight on fasting:

> Moreover, when you fast, do not be like the hypo-
> crites, with a sad countenance. For they disfigure

their faces that they may appear to men to be fasting.
Assuredly, I say to you, they have their reward.

—MATTHEW 6:16, NKJV

You must fast with the right motivation. If you fast only to bring attention to yourself, or only for the physical results you hope to achieve, it has become nothing more than another idol in your life.

You must choose between the reward of man and the reward of God. A fast that is focused on self is rewarded by man, but a broken and contrite heart is rewarded by God.

You may be reading this and thinking, "Sounds great, but who has the time?" I do believe we all need to take stock and see if there are ways we can simplify our lives. You may have too much on your plate and this is your wake-up call to set some boundaries. But the point I'm making is that if you reserve fasting only for the times when you can physically leave or lock yourself away, you will not fast.

I've raised four sons. I understand the very real season of life when your children have legitimate demands on your time. When I was in the middle of that season God didn't tell me to check into a hotel room. He probably knew I would pass out and sleep the whole time! He wanted me to develop the ability to fast within my home and lifestyle.

God wants to be an integral part of your life every day, not just when you are on the mountain spiritually or when everything in your life is calm and quiet. You have to develop a listening ear, one that can hear amid the din and noise of a full household or a hectic schedule. I learned to listen while I took a shower, washed the dishes, and sorted laundry.

This may surprise you, but most of my time on my knees is spent emptying my heart and repenting. Once this is done, I can usually hear God's voice whenever He desires to speak to me. When I prepare to speak at a conference or event, I study and make pages of notes. Often I never use them. I make notes for my sake, to put my mind at ease. The real preparation comes when I confess and cleanse my heart before the Lord.

This time of cleansing allows the Holy Spirit to flow through me. It separates the precious and holy (God's Word and anointing) from the vile (my agenda or prejudice). I separate myself physically for whatever time it takes until I sense this separation has taken place spiritually.

DIETING VS. FASTING

In the weeks leading up to my wedding God told me *not to diet*—then He told me *to fast*. This would seem a contradiction; both are a restriction of food. The difference lies in the purpose or motive that inspires them. A diet is designed to help you lose or gain weight. A change of diet may also be initiated to improve or correct health problems. Dieting is a natural physical application that alters our physical well-being, weight, or health. It changes the way we *look* or *feel*.

Fasting is not for weight gain or loss. Nor is it limited to natural healing. It is not designed to change the way you look and feel but to change the way you *perceive and live.* *A diet may change the way you look, but a fast will change the way you live.* A diet may change your appearance, but a fast will change the way you see; it will alter your inner perspective. The world has perverted and reduced the fast, diminishing it to a diet. As such, it is not a spiritual renewal but a physical one. The deepest transformations are wrought from the inside out.

Before my confrontation with truth, I'd only fasted to lose weight. Granted, I might have done a combination fast and diet, using reasoning such as this: "I need to lose weight, and I need direction, so I'll fast and accomplish both." But on this type of fast, food and weight are still the focus. I have searched the Scriptures and found no reference in God's Word to a fast prescribed for weight loss. Your focus or motive on a fast will be your reward. If God isn't the center, it will be reduced to merely a time of denial.

The fast God led me to in the weeks prior to my wedding was not really about *food* at all—it was about *faith*. I previously placed my faith in my weight. During my fast I learned to transfer my dependency to God. I wanted to know Him; I wanted His truth in my innermost being. *I wanted transformation—not weight reduction.*

Some of you do not need to lose weight, but you do need to break the tethers of a weight that has a hold upon you. *You do not need to lose weight—you need to be loosed from the weight!*

For too long you've measured yourself by images of the

"ideal" person or lifestyle, allowing unhealthy comparisons to affect your moods and actions. You haven't been Spirit-led—you've been weight-led, food-led, emotion-led, addiction-led, or comparison-led. You've been "idol-led."

I was weighed down by weight. My fast was not the turning point for my weight loss; it was the turning point of my faith. I had trusted in myself, only to be disappointed. I needed a spiritual and emotional overhaul. When I saw my idolatry:

> I wept and chastened my soul with fasting.
>
> —PSALM 69:10, NKJV

It is your soul that gives an idol preeminence. My soul confused slim with success. My soul longed for my father's approval and for the approval of men. My soul distorted my vision and perceptions until my physical size, shape, and weight dominated my thought life. I allowed my soul to lead me away from truth and moderation. My soul had to be chastened, and I had to be the one to do it. I had to rise up in the spirit and subject my soul to a chastening fast.

To *chasten* is to "discipline, purify, refine, clarify, and improve." Discipline is training, and I had to be reprogrammed. Chastening was necessary to educate and cultivate a new me. This chastening by fasting began a purification and refinement of my soul and motives. This clarification brought insight so I could once again see clearly. Just as parents discipline their children to help them grow and learn right from wrong, my soul had to be chastened so it could improve and become wiser.

This refinement of my soul worked its way out and overtook my natural body and appetites. It was refined and purified by denial. Once the cravings of my soul were mastered, the cravings of my flesh followed. I was no longer enflamed with a passion for food. My body was denied salt and sugar, and their use came back into balance.

When I could no longer comfort myself with food, I ran to God for comfort. I recovered the lost time and productivity I had lent to my obsession with food and weight. All the hours of research and study were redirected. I had been relieved of the relentless burden of worry and fear over my weight. I felt the lightness of a captive set free from a hard and unforgiving taskmaster. My efforts were never good enough before, and I was never thin enough.

My emotions tipped back into balance. They were no longer tied to the fragile and fickle red arrow of my scale.

Before, I had hated myself when I was fat and loved myself when I was thin. My whole self-image could be shattered with the slightest changing of the indicator on my scale. My sense of worth was dictated by the opinions or reactions of others to my physical shape. Even when I was thin I was tormented by fear. The obsession caused me to live on the edge of extreme elation or deep depression. I was at the mercy of the scale and public opinion.

Fasting changed my perception by changing my focus. This in turn caused me to change the way I lived. I didn't live for food or weight; I lived for God. I saw things differently.

Just as people experience increased clarity of eyesight during a physical fast, on my spiritual fast I had my spiritual eyes stripped of scales that had blinded them.

After the fast my eyes were illuminated by God's Word and truth. My eyes shifted off me and onto my Father God. I could see the right path on which to walk, and I recognized my former errors in judgment. Fasting gave me a new vision and a new direction for my life. Like David, when I humbled myself with fasting (Ps. 35:13) I brought my soul and, inevitably, my body under subjection to God's Word and truth. Before that I had been in submission to the cravings and appetites of my flesh and soul.

> I proclaimed a fast, so that we might humble ourselves before our God and ask him for a safe journey for us and our children, with all our possessions.
>
> —Ezra 8:21

Fasting positions you to acknowledge God's provision in your life. It communicates that He is your source. You deny yourself food and tell Him, "I only want You and what You provide." When you lay aside the daily routine of food, drink, pleasures, and leisure, you are able to reevaluate your priorities.

Fasting is not about food; it is about separation. This separation represents a consecration to the Lord, a change in our relationship with Him. God posed this question to Israel:

> Is this the kind of fast I have chosen, only a day for a man to humble himself? Is it only for bowing

one's head like a reed and for lying on sackcloth and ashes? Is that what you call a fast, a day acceptable to the LORD?

Is not this the kind of fasting I have chosen: to *loose* the *chains* of injustice and *untie* the *cords* of the yoke, to *set* the oppressed *free* and break every yoke? Is it not to *share* your food with the *hungry* and to *provide* the poor wanderer with *shelter*— when you see the *naked*, to *clothe* him, and not to turn away from your own flesh and blood?

Then your *light* will break forth like the dawn, and your *healing* will quickly appear; then your *righteousness* will go before you, and the *glory of the Lord* will be your rear *guard*. Then you will call, and the LORD will *answer*; you will cry for *help*, and he will say: Here am I.

If you do away with the yoke of oppression, with the pointing finger and malicious talk, and if you *spend yourselves* in behalf of the hungry and satisfy the needs of the oppressed…Then your light will rise in the darkness, and your night will become like the noonday. The LORD will guide you always; he will satisfy your needs in a sun-scorched land and will strengthen your frame. You will be like a well-watered garden, like a spring whose waters never fail.

—ISAIAH 58:5–11,
emphasis added

The Israelites' fast had been reduced to religious motions and the denial of food. God was saying that they had reduced it to a one-day happening; they had lost the substance behind the fast. They had lost contact with God's heart on the matter. God imparts His outlook by outlining the fast that pleases Him.

The fast God chooses loosens chains, unties cords, sets free, breaks every yoke, puts you in a position to share and provide for others, and turns your heart toward the needs of your own flesh and blood. God did not want a single day set aside occasionally to honor Him. He wanted a radical and profound change in lifestyle.

If you aren't careful, you can fast for the wrong reasons. Fasting without pure intentions can become an idol. You must know *why* you are fasting. The Israelites were experts in the law but not in love. They turned from the poor and from doing good. God told His people that if they would reach out beyond themselves, everything they had tried to get for themselves would be provided to them. You can dare to reach out beyond yourself because He promises to bring His light to your darkness, to heal you, and to make you righteous. His glory will guard you, and He will answer your prayers and help you in your time of need.

God wants you to do away with the yoke of oppression. In my case, an eating disorder was the yoke. Such yokes are always oppressive—to those who bear them and to those around them. Likewise, addictions are a yoke of oppression, and so are out-of-control emotions such as anger, anxiety, and fear.

God is admonishing us to get our eyes off ourselves, to stop comparing and contrasting ourselves with others—whether we feel superior or inferior by comparison. For too long we have spent all our time and energy on the needs of ourselves, but God wants us to spend ourselves on the needs of others, to lift those who are oppressed.

If you'll commit to a time of fasting, God can make it a turning point. He wants your focus to shift permanently from yourself to others. This means a departure from the realm of self-consciousness to an existence free from selfish motives, thus grasping God's heart.

ROOM FOR MORE

How can you be sure fasting food is the right decision? Ask yourself:

- *In the past, how have I viewed fasting?*

- *How often do I diet? Do I see fasting as a way of dieting?*

- *Have my previous fasts been done with the desire for a turning point or answers?*

- *While reading this chapter, did I feel a desire to fast?*

If your answers were positive, then I believe the Holy Spirit is calling you to enter a deeper level in your walk with God. Separate yourself to Him. Ask God to reveal the influences and areas that stand as hindrances between you and a deeper relationship with Him. Write down some of your motives and prayer requests before you begin your fast.

Even if denying yourself food is a painful process, you will soon discover you have an appetite for something better. If you remain full, even the honey of God's wisdom will seem unappetizing (Prov. 27:7). Just like a second round of dessert after you have already eaten a Thanksgiving banquet, what looked so good at the beginning of the meal now causes you to groan in discomfort just looking at it.

I believe you are hungry, and that is why you are giving the gift of your time in order to read this book. I believe you want more than what you've had and are therefore willing to give more of yourself to God.

Fasting is not a burden but a privilege. It is intimate and private. It originated in the secret place between you and God. He waits in the secret place for you to join Him. After you visit with Him in secret, He will reward you openly.

God wants to restore order where there has been disorder. He wants us to fast so we can be transformed. *Inward transformation brings about outward anointing, blessing, and provision.* Inward transformation positions you for the promotion of the Lord. Even in the midst of opposition, if you fast as an act of separation from the world and unto God, He will reward you.

Chapter 8

TEARING DOWN IDOLS

What you see and what you hear depends a good deal on where you are standing. It also depends on what sort of person you are.[1]

—C. S. Lewis

THE HISTORY OF Israel's relationship with God is an example of our spiritual walk with God. We can look at the strengths and weaknesses of the Israelites and learn from them. Whenever one of the kings of Israel or Judah set his heart to serve God and walk in His righteous commands, God would hear the people's prayers and restore and deliver them from their enemies. But often the very next generation found themselves right back in idolatry. They'd witnessed firsthand the miraculous deliverance of God whenever they returned to Him. They knew His mighty works and power. They knew His righteous judgment on their sin and unbelief, yet it seems they were bent on repeating the idolatry of their fathers.

A TALE OF TWO KINGS

This cycle repeated itself again and again throughout Israel's history. Why? Because though there had been repentance, idols remained in their land. King Jehoshaphat is an example of this:

> In everything he walked in the ways of his father Asa and did not stray from them; he did what was right in the eyes of the LORD. *The high places, however, were not removed, and the people continued to offer sacrifices and burn incense there.* Jehoshaphat was also at peace with the king of Israel.
>
> —1 KINGS 22:43–44,
> *emphasis added*

Though Jehoshaphat did not stray, he did not pave the way for others. He did not clear a path for his people or the son who would follow him. So the people continued in their idolatry. With the high places intact, the spirit of idolatry never left. It remained among the people. Jehoshaphat was also at peace with the king of Israel. During his reign, the kings of Israel were wicked, and this peace was forged through compromises with wickedness.

It was not up to the people to tear down the high places—that was for the king to do. His eyes were enlightened. He knew the difference between the truth and a lie. He clearly saw the spiritual forces of wickedness and the power of God. He possessed the authority and power necessary to pull down the high places, but, alas, he did not.

For the sake of a righteous king, Israel was delivered from enemy attacks from without. But inside the kingdom a war was waged on the battleground of compromise—one fought between the righteous remnant and their enemy, the wicked majority. Israel's spiritual bondage remained intact. The blind cannot safely lead the blind; only those with sight can lead.

> Leave them; they are blind guides. If a blind man leads a blind man, both will fall into a pit.
>
> —Matthew 15:14

It is the responsibility of those who see to direct. Hezekiah was a king with foresight. Here is the description of his spiritual reign over Judah:

> He did what was right in the eyes of the LORD, just
> as his *father David* had done. *He removed the high
> places*, smashed the sacred stones and cut down the
> Asherah poles. He broke into pieces the bronze
> snake Moses had made, for up to that time the
> Israelites had been burning incense to it. (It was
> called Nehushtan.)
>
> —2 KINGS 18:3–4,
> *emphasis added*

How interesting. Hezekiah was not as direct a descendant of David as Jehoshaphat was—he was even further removed. Yet Hezekiah earned this distinction because he served God with all his heart just as David had done. Therefore God awarded him David's lineage. Jehoshaphat received the heritage of his natural father, Asa, while Hezekiah received the heritage of his spiritual father, David. Hezekiah was valiant for the Lord. He tore down the idols of the people, even the serpent Moses had fashioned in obedience to God. The king recognized people had idolized even what God had done. I'm sure he was not necessarily popular with the people for his actions, but he was popular with God.

Not only did Hezekiah do what was right, but he also held fast to the Lord and never ceased to follow him (2 Kings 18:5–7). This set him apart and above all the other kings of Judah. The highest honor given him—the one that distinguished him as a righteous king—was the fact that "the Lord was with him." God was alongside him, making sure any undertaking of his would be successful.

In contrast with Jehoshaphat, Hezekiah would not make peace with or pay tribute to the king of Assyria. This king represented the height of evil and arrogance in his time. Hezekiah refused to succumb to his threats and intimidation, even though he had destroyed every other nation that rebelled against him.

YOUR ROYAL AUTHORITY

If you don't tear down the high places, you will find yourself continuing to serve and pay tribute to your idols. You might question, "But I'm not a king. I'm not even in a place of leadership. What can I do? How can I possibly tear down any high places?"

Have you not repented? Do you not have sight? Have you not been given authority, power, and position?

Not only is a kingly anointing on your life, but you also possess a priestly anointing. (See Revelation 1:5–6.) Now tear down the high places. Though you may not possess authority in a natural earthly kingdom, you do in the heavenlies. God has equipped you with power and authority. Read that last sentence again! Let it sink into your spirit. You have the delegated authority of the Son of God; you have His Word; you have been washed in His blood; and He has all glory and dominion forever!

You have been granted a view high above all present deception and darkness. Your eyes have been enlightened by the Truth—and He has set you free. Refuse to pay homage, tribute, or honor to idols any longer. Stand strong, and do not be entangled again with the yoke of slavery (Gal. 5:1).

Do you know you can be set free and then become encumbered again? You can be free in Christ and entangled again with the yoke of religion. You can be free in Christ and entangled again with the world. To remain free in Christ, take a regular inventory and remove every religious or worldly influence.

ALIENS AND STRANGERS

If we're honest we would find that many of us long to look like the children of the world. If we could just have their image and God too! The problem: we have allowed the image of the world to be imprinted upon us more deeply than the image of Christ.

As you read this book you are surrounded by the light of truth. The things I bring before you I bring to you in the presence of this light. It is not my objective to be judgmental or critical, though what I say might sound so at first. Please hear it in the light of the truth, because the lie has permeated the church for far too long.

I am not addressing the *lost in the world*; I am addressing the *confused in the church*. Why are so many Christians conforming to the image of this world? Why do we consult their periodicals on how to dress, how to wear our makeup or tone our bodies, and how to find a woman or man? Why do we watch hours of their adulterous and seductive entertainment at movies and on TV? What image are we conforming to?

We know the image the world is serving, but what image is the church serving? Are we striving to be sexually attractive? Do we fan the wrong fire? Are we believers or not? Are we aspiring to be like the world in order to win the world's acceptance? Does acceptance by the world bring the lost into the kingdom?

I believe the Book of James gives us a definite answer:

> Adulterers and adulteresses! Do you not know that friendship with the world is enmity with God? Whoever therefore wants to be a friend of the world makes himself an enemy of God. Or do you think that the Scripture says in vain, "The Spirit who dwells in us yearns jealously?"
>
> —James 4:4–5, nkjv

How much clearer does it need to be? For too long our goal has been to become like the world so they could embrace us. No! They are not to embrace us. They are to embrace Christ. We are to live in such a way that *He* is lifted up (John 12:32). We are called to declare truth in the midst of a lost and dying world. Peter warned the believers of his day this way:

> Dear friends, I urge you, as foreigners and exiles in the world, to abstain from sinful desires, which war against your soul.
>
> —1 Peter 2:11

Do aliens and strangers *conform* or *stand out*? The world understands why they need outward transformation: this

present life is all they live for. They adorn themselves outwardly to hide their inward emptiness. It confuses them
when Christians who have supposedly experienced inward
transformation focus as much as they do on the outward.
We are to tell them about *our* world, not long to fit in with
theirs. We are to come out and be separate, not blend in.

The first part of declaring truth is to live it. When I was
tearing down the idol of distorted body image I removed
all the *Glamour*, *Harper's Bazaar*, *Vogue*, *Self*, *Fit*, and
Victoria's Secret catalogs from my house. After all, did I
really want my sons to begin to think these were the types
of women they should desire? Do you want your daugh-
ters turning to these sources for advice? I put their images
away from me. I refused to buy their subscriptions or order
their products.

As a family, we refused most of the cable channels and
turned off the TV. This tuned out the seductive imagery
that, though it lasts but a second, imprints its image upon
the canvas of my mind and the minds of those I love.

> And what union can there be between God's temple
> and idols? For we are the temple of the living God.
> As God said: "I will live in them and walk among
> them. I will be their God, and they will be my
> people. Therefore, come out from them and sepa-
> rate yourselves from them, says the Lord. Don't
> touch their filthy things and I will welcome you."
>
> —2 Corinthians 6:16–18, NLT

Do you want to be a vessel entrusted to carry the precious Spirit of God? Then you must come out and be separate. This means purging yourself of the filthiness of the flesh so you can shine as a beacon and speak the true words of God. You must tear down spiritual darkness by the power of an obedient life.

You will not find lasting worth in anything but God.

Chapter 9

ESCAPING YOUR PAST

Reject your sense of injury and the injury itself disappears.[1]

—MARCUS AURELIUS

There's a reason I spent so much of this book sharing a painful season from my past. I'm sure you have painful things in your past too. If not, just live a little longer. You can't get very far in this life without experiencing pain, making mistakes, and having regrets.

But I believe too many people use the past as an excuse or justification for present behavior. I have already addressed the idolatry of serving a worldly image. When you make excuses for yourself by drawing from your past, that too is idolatry. Remember, an idol is what you give your strength to or draw your strength from.

Some people spend their strength and selves in the research of their own pasts. They study it, looking for a reason and rhyme for their life. They may think their past justifies their present, but the truth is that the past will never justify the future.

There are those who look intently into the mirror of their lives, hoping its reflection will hold answers for them. This is deception. We will never change by beholding ourselves. James describes this condition:

> Do not merely listen to the word, and so deceive yourselves. Do what it says. Anyone who listens to the word but does not do what it says is like a man who looks at his face in a mirror and, after looking at himself, goes away and immediately forgets what he looks like. But the man who looks intently into the perfect law that gives freedom, and continues to

do this, not forgetting what he has heard, but doing
it—he will be blessed in what he does.

—JAMES 1:22–25

James is saying that you are not to be the focus. Your
focus is to be the perfect law of liberty. It will give you
the freedom you seek. You are forgetful when you only
hear the Word and do not also obey it. Part of obedience is applying God's truth to your life and circumstances. If you do not do this, you will find yourself open
to self-deception.

NEARSIGHTEDNESS

Second Peter 1:5–9 gives an outline for the healthy development of Christian attributes. First you add goodness to
your measure of faith. This includes believing that God
is a *good God*. Next you add knowledge to this revelation
of goodness, and to knowledge, you add self-control. To
this, you add perseverance; to perseverance, you add godliness; to godliness, you add brotherly kindness; and lastly,
to brotherly kindness, you add love.

You are promised that if you "possess these qualities in
increasing measure, they will keep you from being inef-
fective and unproductive in your knowledge of our Lord
Jesus Christ" (2 Peter 1:8). These are all measures that can
be increased by use and the exercise of your faith.

We are also warned, "But whoever does not have [these
qualities] is nearsighted and blind, forgetting that they
have been cleansed from their past sins" (v. 9).

Nearsighted and blind people have a hard time seeing things accurately. I know; I'm nearsighted. Without the help of my glasses, I do not recognize the form of my own husband until he is within twenty feet of me.

Impaired eyesight causes loss of insight. The near-sighted only notice the obvious. Often the obvious overshadows the eternal. This shortsighted condition makes you forgetful: "Where did I leave my keys?" If the item is not right in front of you, you quickly forget it. Peter said such a condition will cause us to forget we have been cleansed. When this knowledge is lost, we begin to make excuses.

Like I said earlier, if we do not obey the truth that has been clearly revealed, we will deceive ourselves. (See James 1.) Our hearts will condemn us if we attempt to make justification for our sins by the works of the flesh and psychology of man. Let's go back to the purpose of salvation. Was it not to restore us to God through the remission of sins and the removal of our past?

When I stand before God I will stand alone as an individual. Each of us will be judged for what we have done. That is why I need a Savior. I had lived a life that could not stand the scrutiny and presence of a holy God. I became a Christian when I experienced this revelation: I was sinful, and God was holy. The two could never touch. Jesus became my Mediator.

Job described his need for a savior this way:

> If only there were someone to arbitrate between us,
> to lay his hand upon us both.
> —JOB 9:33

OUR MEDIATOR

We have that Someone. He mediates between us and God. Picture this: You stand before God's eternal throne. The Book of Life is opened, and the written code against you is read aloud for all to hear. You cower under the weight of your sins in the presence of this holy Judge. Your sins are so filthy and the list so immense and far-reaching that you tremble and fear that you are unforgivable.

Your only hope is your glorious Advocate, the Judge's only Son. You weep and tremble in the silence that proceeds the pronouncement of your judgment: "You are guilty as charged." The finality and terror of this verdict grip you as an angel steps forward to escort you out.

Then your Advocate steps forward and pleads your cause. "Father, You are just to pronounce her guilty. She knew this day would come, and she traded her sin-riddled life for My lordship. She has been My servant. My death satisfies the written judgment against her. The sins she has committed are under the covering of My blood."

"Forgiven," the Judge pronounces.

Now you are free! Imagine your relief and joy! Once and for eternity, you have been judged worthy of citizenship in God's kingdom—not because of what you did or the life you lived, not because of what others thought of you or how you measured up to them, but because of what Jesus did. His righteousness is above question, and it has been assigned to you!

Now imagine a different court scene. Again, the list of sins is read, and the defendant is found guilty. The

Advocate comes before the Judge and says, "Guilty as charged, but I have shed My blood to pay her debt." This time the defendant despises this extension of mercy.

She stands up and begins to justify her own actions. The Mediator rushes to her side and cautions, "If you make your own defense, I can no longer be your Mediator."

But she proceeds in her own foolish defense: "It is not my fault; you don't know what they did to me! Get my parents in here; it is *their* fault!" Or, "I was hurt and rejected; that is why I acted so hatefully. It is the fault of *those who hurt me*!"

The Mediator answers, "They have already been judged. They are not on trial here; *you* are."

"Well, I know I did all those things, but it was not my fault. I'll make my own defense. It's not fair!"

Though her guilt can be blotted from God's sight, when she justifies it she keeps it on the record. She loses her Mediator and now stands before the breach between a holy God and her own sinful human nature.

What do you think this woman's sentence will be? She will be judged guilty, of course. Guilty of sin, unforgiveness, unbelief, and irreverence—to name a few. She will also be guilty of treating Christ's precious sacrifice as common. She will be judged not by the mercy of the new covenant but by the law. For it is the law that says, "An eye for an eye"; in more common terms, "You did this to me, so I did this to you; it's your fault."

This may seem preposterous to you, but it is not. When you excuse yourself, you stand before God in your own righteousness. That righteousness is as filthy rags. Your defense cannot be compiled based on the reasons and motives behind what you did.

You are not justified by what was done *to* you; you are justified by what was done *for* you. You are not even justified by any good works you have done. Your sole justification is faith in Christ's sacrifice. You may be rewarded like a faithful servant for what you have done, but you will not be excused by it.

YOUR PAST IS NOT YOUR FUTURE

Therefore, if anyone is in Christ, the new creation has come: The old has gone, the new is here!
—2 Corinthians 5:17

Are you in Christ? Then you *must* let go of the old. It is gone, and a new way of living has been prepared for you. You must use your gift of faith to step into this new life. Let go of your past, because *your past is not your future.*

God is the Lord of your future. He sees your potential, not your current circumstances. He has plans for you. He is always planning ahead so you don't have to. All you have to do is trust Him and learn His ways. His ways are higher and wiser, and He clearly tells you to forget your past.

Philippians 3:13–14 says to forget what is behind. It exhorts you to strain for what is ahead, loosing yourself of the load of your past. That is the only way you can have the necessary strength to persevere to your goal.

How many marathon runners carry backpacks? If a

runner started with one, it would soon be dropped in order to lighten her load so she could finish her race. Marathon runners compete in the lightest apparel possible and carry only what is necessary for their journey. The marathon runner knows she must conserve all her strength for the race at hand.

You also run a race:

> The path of the righteous is like the morning sun, shining ever brighter till the full light of day.
>
> —PROVERBS 4:18

The path becomes clearer and more distinct as you walk it. As long as you go forward, your light will increase. You travel out of darkness by keeping His light ahead. Looking back will do you no good. You can't go forward when you are looking back, so you must turn to the Son and follow His light. With each step, you leave the realm of darkness and travel deeper into His light, until it shines brighter than the full light of day.

Some of you are running with backpacks filled with stones because you are trying to bring your past into the future. Others of you are looking back. Maybe you are afraid your future will be like your past. Now is the time to put the past to rest.

When you excuse your behavior by your past, you say, "I've earned the right to be this way because of what was done to me." This attitude betrays the presence of unforgiveness in your heart. Forgiveness is the very foundation of the gospel. Without forgiveness, there is no remission of sin. Unforgiveness will keep you bound to your past.

> Do not judge, and you will not be judged. Do not condemn, and you will not be condemned. Forgive, and you will be forgiven.
>
> —Luke 6:37

Unforgiveness inevitably causes you to lose sight of your own need of forgiveness. You have God's promise that if you forgive, you will be forgiven. It is when you don't forgive that the weight of your own sins comes back to bear down on you. The forgiveness of God is the very force that releases you from your past. You can even release others, for "if you forgive anyone his sins, they are forgiven; if you do not forgive them, they are not forgiven" (John 20:23). But remember, by not forgiving others, you are also not forgiven. Some of you have withheld forgiveness as a form of punishment when in the end you are only punishing yourselves. Is it worth it?

THE POWER OF FORGIVENESS

When we were first married, John did something that really hurt me. It happened a few times. Each time John came to me afterward and apologized. But I would reject his apology.

"I'll believe you are sorry *when you change!*"

This response was safe for me. It meant that I did not have to extend forgiveness to John until he had proven himself worthy of it. This pattern continued for a while.

Each time John hurt me, I felt more justified in with-holding my forgiveness. He would apologize, and, out of my hurt, I would lash out.

"I *knew* you weren't sorry! *You did it again*! I don't even want to hear your apology!"

I was bitter and tormented because I had never extended forgiveness. It happened again; now I was mad at God *and* John. I went to prayer and asked the Lord to change my husband, and here is how the Holy Spirit answered:

"John will not be able to change *until you forgive him*."

"I don't believe he is sorry," I argued. "If he were, he would stop it! Why is everything always my responsibility? Why do I always have to be the one to change? I'm the one who is getting hurt!"

"Tell John you believe he wants to change and that you forgive him."

God had issued some very clear directives to me without once commenting on John's behavior. I had wanted Him to judge John, maybe speak to him in a dream and scare the daylights out of him. God wasn't interested in my solu-tion. Instead, He presented me with some options. Now I had the choice to obey His command to forgive and release John, or to disobey and retain his offense.

I had been taught that the way you proved you were sorry was by changing. God was challenging me to extend mercy to John when I didn't think he had earned it. That is the beauty of mercy. It cannot be earned, and it is given when we least deserve it because that is when we most need it.

I went to John and shared with him what God had told me. I apologized for punishing him with my unforgiveness. I had done it to protect myself and had wound up hurting us both. Once I was obedient, the power of God was released into our situation, and healing and restoration took place.

That was a moment of truth for me, and I would face many more. Some of them caused me to take stock of my heart, and I discovered that I didn't always like what I found there. I wanted to blame someone else. Then I would not be so uncomfortable because I would not be responsible for my own actions. Right?

I did this for a while, hoping it would make me feel better. I had forgotten that by bringing up the pasts of others, I was also dredging up my own. I had forgotten that if I held my loved ones accountable for their pasts, then God would have to hold me accountable for mine. Remember that He uses the same measure and method of judgment to judge us that we have used to judge others.

We cannot pick and choose the application of Scriptures to our own liking. We are quick to defend ourselves when the devil brings up our past: "That's covered by Jesus's blood!" If this is true—and it is—then why would we ever resurrect it ourselves?

We do it to defend ourselves. Our self-defense is just as foolish in the courts of earth as it would seem in heaven. "You know, I came from a dysfunctional family. That is why I can't help it. It's just the way I am." No, that is the way you were before you got saved. No longer are you to continue to live and conduct yourself in the same way. Too often we think that the abuse we suffered in the past grants us a special exception in the present. We have convinced ourselves that we do not need to change because God understands that ours is a special case, as if Jesus's death were not enough to heal and restore us. The truth is, it is enough. No matter how painful the past, its hold on you was annihilated by the cross.

DON'T LOOK BACK!

No one who puts a hand to the plow and looks back
is fit for service in the kingdom of God.

—Luke 9:62

Looking back makes you unfit for kingdom service. You must again place your hands firmly on the plow and push forward. If you look back while you plow, your rows will be uneven, and you run the danger of breaking your plow blades on rocks or stumps. Plowing requires a constant eye fixed on what is immediately ahead in the field.

The past is gone. It is dead. When you allow your focus to be diverted backward, you forget that you have been cleansed, and you start to make excuses.

Now it is time to change your focus. It is time to let go. *You are not what you have done. You are not what has been done to you. You have been translated from that dark domain onto God's path of light.* Your worth is not found in *what you have done.* It is represented by *what Jesus did for you.* If you really believe what He did was enough to wash away your sins, then you must acknowledge that it was enough to wipe out your past. There are no special cases. No longer are you a person with a past. You are a child of God with a future.

Are you ready? Ask yourself:

- *What are some feelings, thoughts, or experiences from my past that I know I need to let go of?*

- *What memories and fears of my past keep creeping into my present life? How does this infiltrate the future God has for me?*

- *Am I nearsighted, spiritually speaking? Why or why not?*

If you are ready to escape your past, and if you realize that your past is not your future, pray this prayer with me:

Father,

Forgive me for using my past to justify my present. Jesus, I embrace You as my justification and righteousness. I choose to walk in newness of life and turn my eyes off myself and onto Your Word. I will not be a hearer only. I will be a doer. Then my discernment will remain clear and accurate. I rise up out of the dust of my past. I leave behind me all the bondage of guilt and fear. From this day forward I have no past. I will not look back at it. I go forward. In Jesus's name, amen.

Chapter 10

WHAT YOU SEE

Of all the senses, sight must be the most delightful.[1]

—HELEN KELLER

Independent of our marital, professional, or social status, our talents and abilities are not to be used to serve ourselves but to serve others. We each have an opportunity to serve God in our unique sphere of influence. God plants each of us in various soils to accomplish His purpose.

> Love each other deeply, because love covers over a multitude of sins…Each of you should use whatever gift you have received to serve others, as faithful stewards of God's grace in its various forms.
>
> —1 Peter 4:8–10

The world is preaching an opposing gospel. Almost without exception, the covers of secular magazines boast young, attractive, seductive men and women and promise to reveal the secrets to great sex, constant good looks, and guaranteed success. All of these are meant to entice subscribers with self-gratification. They offer slavery to the lust of this world, while God offers servitude. Their message: live for the moment, live for pleasure, and live for yourself!

But what is the message of Christ? How can those of us who know the truth help spread the truth?

If you're like most people, on some level you have conformed to the world's images and lies. Your actions and lifestyle validated them. Now that you have turned your back on the lies, you need to find your purpose. Letting go of lies can be frightening until truth is revealed. In obedience you have renounced the lies and their idolatries; now you need to glean the precious from the vile. You were led astray because you were looking—no, longing—for someone to define you.

WHO ARE YOU?

I remember my freshman year in college. There was the pretend me and the real me, the projected image and the protected one. But it was not long before the distinctions began to blur. The projected me was so busy trying to win approval and give the appearance of strength that I soon forgot who I really was, who it was I was protecting. As this progressed, I didn't like being alone. I wanted to be in a constant social setting. If you couldn't show me a good time, I didn't want to be around you. I was shallow and thoughtless. I was nothing more than what you saw. Like so many, I'd conformed to a cultural image and felt empty and lost.

My own fear of failure and desire for approval from men drove me to live a lie. I chose to allow those around me to define me. I could blame my father, boyfriends, a painful past, or brazen cultural influences, but the truth is, I had been void of truth, so I embraced lies.

Until I met Jesus, *the Truth* was not in me. I had to spurn the man-made information to embrace transformation. Transformation could only come by renewing my mind, by reading God's Word. This meant I had to leave behind my former ways.

Many of you were already acquainted with Jesus when you began this book. But in this area of image, you were more acquainted with the message of the world than the message of Christ. I believe as you have read this book, you've recognized and repented of these sympathies. This has released and empowered you to walk in truth. It is my prayer that you will never be entangled again. You've been untethered from the lie; now I want you bound to truth.

Jesus is that truth. As you live and apply His truth, you will walk on the path of ever-increasing light. Recall the words of Proverbs 4:18:

> The path of the righteous is like the first gleam of dawn, shining ever brighter till the full light of day.

The prayers and steps you've taken in good faith have placed your feet on the path of righteousness. At the first gleam of dawn, the light is dim, but as you continue toward the light of His Word it grows brighter.

The psalmist said, "Thy word is a lamp unto my feet, and a light unto my path" (Psalm 119:105, KJV). Your understanding is illuminated as you read God's Word. It is important to approach the Word with humility. There is danger when you go to the Word to gather information that will establish your opinions or beliefs. You then read what you believe instead of believing what you read. When you go to the Word with a teachable, meek, and humble heart, you are transformed. Dim eyes are flooded with the light of spiritual wisdom and understanding for the revelation of God.

> I pray that your hearts will be flooded with light so that you can understand the wonderful future

he has promised to those he called. I want you to realize what a rich and glorious inheritance he has given to his people.

—Ephesians 1:18, nlt

Christ embodies every dream and hope, not only in heaven but also as an inheritance for you on earth. He gives you purpose, plans, and a future. His death defines your life.

Set your minds on things above, not on earthly things. For you died, and your life is now hidden with Christ in God. When Christ, who is your life, appears, then you also will appear with him in glory.

—Colossians 3:2–4,
emphasis added

He is your life. He is "Christ in you, the hope of glory" (Col. 1:27). Because your life is hidden in Him, your mind, desires, and affections are to be set on things above, not on earthly things.

When Adam and Eve were in the garden, their minds went from the heavenly and eternal to the earthly and temporal. In Christ your focus is restored again to the eternal. By losing sight of the seen you gain the unseen. At the revelation of God's glory you will be seen for what you really are.

At the time of your rebirth you put on a new man (or woman) who is being renewed or regenerated inwardly until it takes on the image of its Creator. You will be restored to the original image God intended for you. No longer will you be formed in the image of culture; you are once again created in the image of God.

When I look at God's holiness, and then look at myself, it seems impossible that I have been created in the image of God! Looking at yourself you can only see what is possible; looking at God you can see the impossible. What is impossible with man is possible with God. You are not to measure what God can do by what you have done. You are not the focus; the possibility of your new image is not based on you but on a victory Christ has already won. It does not matter how many times you may have tried and failed; it is not about you or your ability.

> Do not be afraid; you will not suffer shame. Do not fear disgrace; you will not be humiliated. *You will forget* the shame of your youth and remember no more the reproach of your widowhood.
>
> —Isaiah 54:4,
> *emphasis added*

This promise in Isaiah 54 is God's invitation to leave behind your prison of fear. He assures you that shame and humiliation will not be your future, and He promises to erase all the shameful memories and reproach of your past. This promise is available to each child of God. It is for those who will dare to believe and thereby mix His precious words with faith.

Remember, your past is not your future! God holds out the hope of a future free from the fear of failure. When the woman taken in adultery was brought before Jesus, He told her, "Go, and sin no more" (John 8:11, KJV). Notice He did not say, "I know you have a problem with men because you never had a healthy relationship with your father. I want you to go through six months of counseling, and once you have figured this all out, then you will be able to go and sin no more." Her past did not matter; His forgiveness and word held the power to free her. Looking to the past arouses doubt and reawakens our self-consciousness, thus reducing our *God*-consciousness.

You may say, "It is all too simple." Human nature is often drawn to the difficult and complex, but I find God most often in the pure and simple. You are free. The light has shone on your path. Now the choice is yours. Will you walk in the light?

DEFINED BY GOD

Until God imparted His purpose and plan into my life, I felt entirely purposeless. Your purpose or calling defines you. Jesus defined you with His death.

> You are a chosen people, a royal priesthood, a holy nation, a people belonging to God, that you may declare the praises of him who called you out of darkness into his wonderful light.
>
> —1 PETER 2:9

God defines you because He has chosen you. He separated you from the world to bring you back to Himself. He delivered you out of darkness into the light so that you would declare His praises. You belong to Him, purchased by the priceless blood of His Son.

One of my favorite quotes is: "Until you find something worth dying for, you're not really alive." It would be even more true to say, "Because Jesus thought you were something worth dying for, you can be truly alive." He exchanged His vibrant, abundant life for your gray and lifeless one.

By whose definition will you live?

Pray with me one final time:

> *Father,*
>
> *Redefine my life. I am done conforming to the world's standards. Lord, please transform me. Renew my mind and guide me onto the path of righteousness. Bind me to Jesus, who is Truth. I do not want to just be acquainted with you, Father. I want to know You. I want to see Your beauty and light when I look over my life, but even more so I desire for others to see Your truth through me. I know You are the only way to escape the prison I created for myself. I choose to submit to You, that I might walk in freedom. In Your precious name I pray. Amen.*

SIGNS OF EATING DISORDERS

ANOREXIA NERVOSA

1. Dramatic weight loss

2. Preoccupation with weight, food, calories, fat grams, and dieting

3. Refusal to eat certain foods, progressing to restrictions against whole categories of food (e.g., no carbohydrates, etc.)

4. Frequent comments about feeling "fat" or overweight despite weight loss

5. Anxiety about gaining weight or being "fat"

6. Denial of hunger

7. Development of food rituals (e.g., eating foods in certain orders, excessive chewing, rearranging food on a plate)

8. Consistent excuses to avoid mealtimes or situations involving food

9. Excessive, rigid exercise regimen—despite weather, fatigue, illness, or injury, the need to "burn off" calories taken in

10. Withdrawal from usual friends and activities[1]

BULIMIA NERVOSA

1. Evidence of binge eating, including disappearance of large amounts of food in short periods of time or the existence of wrappers and containers indicating the consumption of large amounts of food

2. Evidence of purging behaviors, including frequent trips to the bathroom after meals, signs and/or smells of vomiting, presence of wrappers or packages of laxatives or diuretics

3. Excessive, rigid exercise regimen—despite weather, fatigue, illness, or injury, the need to "burn off" calories taken in

4. Unusual swelling of the cheeks or jaw area

5. Calluses on the back of the hands and knuckles from self-induced vomiting

6. Discoloration or staining of the teeth

7. Creation of lifestyle schedules or rituals to make time for binge-and-purge sessions

8. Withdrawal from usual friends and activities[2]

NOTES

CHAPTER 1—IT'S NOT ABOUT BEING SEEN, IT'S ABOUT WHAT YOU SEE

1. Research shows that this is a compilation of quotes attributed to Marcus Aurelius, based on his teaching; see also George Long, "The Meditations by Marcus Aurelius," *The Meditations by Marcus Aurelius*, Internet Classics Archive, 2009, http://classics.mit.edu/Antoninus/meditations.12.twelve.html (accessed June 18, 2014).

CHAPTER 2—THE TYRANT

1. BrainyQuote.com, "Victor Hugo Quote," http://www.brainyquote.com/quotes/quotes/v/victorhugo402647.html (accessed June 18, 2014).

CHAPTER 3—THE IMAGE OF THE TRUTH

1. Ralph Waldo Emerson and Brooks Atkinson, *The Essential Writings of Ralph Waldo Emerson* (New York: Modern Library, 2000).
2. James Strong, *Strong's Exhaustive Concordance* (Grand Rapids, MI: Baker Book House, 1979), s. v. "know."

CHAPTER 4—THE IMAGE OF THE LIE

1. Simran Khurana, "Eleanor Roosevelt Quotes," About Education, http://quotations.about.com/od/NotableWomenQuotes/a/Eleanor-Roosevelt-Quotes.htm (accessed June 18, 2014).

2. James Wood, "Amiel Quotes," *Dictionary of Quotations*, Bartleby.com, http://www.bartleby.com/345/authors/11.html (accessed June 18, 2014).

3. *Nelson's Illustrated Bible Dictionary* (Nashville: Thomas Nelson Publishers, 1986), s.v. "idol."

CHAPTER 5—SELF-IMAGE OR SELF-WORSHIP?

1. Rick Warren, *The Purpose-driven Life: What on Earth Am I Here For?* (Grand Rapids, MI: Zondervan, 2002), 265.

CHAPTER 6—THE IDOL TUMBLES

1. William Shakespeare, "Hamlet", act 4, scene 5.

CHAPTER 7—SHARPENING YOUR SPIRITUAL SIGHT

1. BrainyQuote.com, "Jonathan Swift Quotes," http://www.brainyquote.com/quotes/quotes/j/jonathansw122246.html (accessed June 18, 2014).

CHAPTER 8—TEARING DOWN IDOLS

1. C. S. Lewis, *The Chronicles of Narnia: The Magician's Nephew* (New York: Harper Collins, 1955) 76.

CHAPTER 9—ESCAPING YOUR PAST

1. Research shows that this is a compilation of quotes attributed to Marcus Aurelius, based on his teaching; see also George Long, "The Meditations by Marcus Aurelius," *The Meditations by Marcus Aurelius*, Internet Classics Archive, 2009, http://classics.mit.edu/Antoninus/meditations.5.five .html (accessed June 18, 2014).

CHAPTER 10—WHAT YOU SEE

1. *Quotes, Biography, Movies and More!*, "Helen Keller Online," http://www.helenkelleronline.com (accessed June 18, 2014).

APPENDIX

1. National Eating Disorders Association, "Anorexia Nervosa," http://www.nationaleatingdisorders.org/anorexia-nervosa (accessed June 18, 2014).
2. National Eating Disorders Association, "Bulimia Nervosa," http://www.nationaleatingdisorders.org/bulimia-nervosa.

OTHER TITLES BY LISA BEVERE

Be Angry, But Don't Blow It!
Fight Like a Girl
Girls with Swords
Kissed the Girls and Made Them Cry
Lioness Arising
Nurture
Out of Control and Loving It!
The Story of Marriage
The True Measure of a Woman
You Are Not What You Weigh

teach reach rescue

Messenger International®

Connect with Lisa on

UNITED STATES

PO Box 888
Palmer Lake, CO 80133

Toll Free: 800-648-1477
Phone: 719-487-3000
Fax: 719-487-3300

UNITED KINGDOM

PO Box 1066
Hemel Hempstead
Hertfordshire, HP2 7GQ
United Kingdom

Freephone: 0800 9808 933
Outside UK: +44 1442 288 531

AUSTRALIA

PO Box 6444
Rouse Hill Town Centre
Rouse Hill, NSW 2155

MessengerInternational.org

GIRLS WITH SWORDS

HOW TO CARRY YOUR CROSS
LIKE A HERO

Curriculum Includes:
- 8 sessions on 3 DVDs &
  4 CDs (30 minutes each)
- Girls with Swords book
- Fencing Manual study guide
- Sword necklace
- Promotional materials

Worldwide, women are the targets of prejudice, sex trafficking, abuse, and gendercide. A spiritual enemy is seeking to disarm women on every level. In Girls with Swords, Lisa Bevere explains how the Word of God is a sword that should be both studied and wielded. If there ever was a time for women to be armed, it's now.

LIONESS ARISING

Wake Up and Change Your World

Curriculum Includes:
- 8 sessions on 3 DVDs &
  4 CDs (30 minutes each)
- Lioness Arising book
- Safari Guide study guide
- Promotional materials

The lioness is a magnificent image of strength, passion, and beauty. Her presence commands the landscape, protects her young, and empowers the lion. Packed with remarkable insights from nature and a rich depth of biblical references to the lioness, Lioness Arising is a call for women to rise up in strength and number to change their world.

Fight Like *a Girl*
The Power of Being a Woman

You are an answer, not a problem.

Curriculum Includes:
- 12 video sessions on 4 DVDs
  (30 minutes each)
- Fight Like a Girl book
- Devotional workbook
- Promotional materials
  & bookmark
- Makeup bag
- Bracelet: genuine
  Swarovski Austrian crystal

In Fight Like a Girl, Lisa challenges the status quo that a woman needs to fit into the role of a man, and she leads you in the truth of what it means to be a woman. Discover how to express your God-given strengths and fulfill your role in the community, workplace, home, and church. This curriculum will encourage you to find your true potential and realize you are an answer and not a problem.

IS YOUR GRIP ON LIFE SO TIGHT THAT GOD CANNOT WORK OUT HIS PLAN?

LISA BEVERE shares an incredible discovery that helped her let go of her obsession to manage and manipulate everything around her. *Out of Control and Loving It!* takes you on a journey from a lifestyle of fear and disorder to a haven of rest and peace under God's protective wings.

LET GOD HELP YOU RELEASE YOUR BURDENS...